Information Governance for Healthcare Professionals

A Practical Approach

Information Governance for Healthcare Professionals

A Practical Approach

By
Robert F. Smallwood

CRC Press
Taylor & Francis Group
Boca Raton London New York

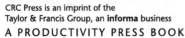

CRC Press is an imprint of the
Taylor & Francis Group, an **informa** business

A PRODUCTIVITY PRESS BOOK

First edition published in 2018
by Routledge/CRC Press
Taylor & Francis Group
6000 Broken Sound Parkway NW, Suite 300
Boca Raton, FL 33487-2742

First issued in paperback 2021

© 2019 by Robert F. Smallwood
CRC Press is an imprint of Taylor & Francis Group, an Informa business

No claim to original U.S. Government works

ISBN 13: 978-1-03-209484-7 (pbk)
ISBN 13: 978-1-138-56806-8 (hbk)

Library of Congress Cataloging-in-Publication Data

Names: Smallwood, Robert F., 1959- author, editor.
Title: Information governance for healthcare professionals : a practical approach / Robert F. Smallwood.
Description: Boca Raton, FL : Taylor & Francis, 2018. | Includes bibliographical references and index.
Identifiers: LCCN 2018020479 (print) | LCCN 2018034858 (ebook) | ISBN 9780203705247 (e-Book) | ISBN 9781138568068 (hardback : alk. paper)
Subjects: LCSH: Medical informatics. | Information resources management.
Classification: LCC R858 (ebook) | LCC R858 .S557 2018 (print) | DDC 610.285--dc23
LC record available at https://lccn.loc.gov/2018020479

Visit the Taylor & Francis Web site at
http://www.taylorandfrancis.com

and the CRC Press Web site at
http://www.crcpress.com

For

Michelli Gil Jaimez

and

Trueman Walker Moore

Gone too soon, they lit up their corner of the world and will forever live in the hearts of all who loved them.

Contents

SECTION II INSIGHTS, STRATEGIES, AND ADVICE FROM THE FIELD

Preface

Healthcare in the United States is at a crossroads; with all the high technology and money that has been thrown at automating electronic health records (EHR) and other aspects of healthcare business operations, the result has been dismal in terms of population health.

Patients in the United States are more likely to die from medical mistakes than in at any of the top 10 civilized nations; in fact, the United States came in dead last in healthcare quality, in a recent study. The United Kingdom, which pioneered information governance (IG) in healthcare, was ranked first in quality, so we felt it appropriate to include some U.K. voices in this book, to bring in some lessons learned and progressive IG perspectives.

IG programs are about minimizing information risks and costs, while maximizing information value. They require a cross-functional effort and collaboration across departments, breaking down traditional operational silos to leverage insights and value across the enterprise.

IG is increasingly seen as a critical organization-wide initiative in well-run healthcare organizations, not only to improve patient care and outcomes, but also as a countermeasure to the growing threats of data breaches and ransomware attacks.

This book is written in a concise, easy-to-read way. It is an action-oriented guide to help healthcare organizations plan and launch successful IG programs. It will help you to develop the business case, form your IG steering committee, develop a program charter, devise metrics, and manage an ongoing IG program. Crystal-clear definitions and concrete steps are presented, which will help organizations worldwide to develop their IG program framework and business objectives, and to measure progress toward achieving them.

Readers will benefit from proven strategies and advice offered by experienced IG practitioners. We hope that benefits can be realized in the near term, and significant improvements in healthcare quality can be made long term, for the good of patients in the United States and worldwide.

Acknowledgments

Thanks to Mark Grysiuk for his editing work early on; to AHIMA for their pioneering work in IG for healthcare organizations; to Kristine Mednansky and HIMSS for supporting this book from the outset, and to the editors at Taylor & Francis/CRC Press for making it a reality; to Richard P. Kessler, Dr. Mansur Hasib, Baird W. Brueseke, Patricia Morris, and Lori Ashley for their fine contributions which helped to explain key issues in healthcare IG; and to Reynold Leming, Andrew Harvey, Barry Moult, and Dennis Kessler for their wonderful insights and perspectives from across the pond!

Author

Robert F. Smallwood, MBA, CIP, IGP, is an industry-leading author, keynote speaker, consultant, and educator. This is his seventh book on Information Governance (IG) topics and he is the world's leading IG author and trainer. Robert is author of the pioneering text *Information Governance: Concepts, Strategies, and Best Practices* (Wiley, 2014, 2019), which is used to guide IG programs at major corporations worldwide and to teach graduate students at universities including Oxford, University of British Columbia, San Jose State, and University of Michigan. Smallwood is a founding partner of IMERGE Consulting and heads up the Institute for Information Governance. He is also Publisher & CEO of *Information Governance World* magazine. In addition to teaching IG courses, he consults with Fortune 500 companies, healthcare organizations, major law firms, and governments. Some of his past research and consulting clients include the U.S. FDA, Ochsner Health System, Baton Rouge General, Novartis Pharmaceuticals, Abbott Labs, Sandia Labs, Sidley Austin LLP, Kirkland & Ellis LLP, and Johnson & Johnson. Mr. Smallwood has published more than 120 articles, published 10 books, and given more than 60 conference presentations. He is also the author of *Information Governance for Executives* (Bacchus, 2016), *Introduction to Information Governance* (Bacchus, 2016), *Managing Electronic Records: Methods, Best Practices, and Technologies* (Wiley, 2013); *Safeguarding Critical E-Documents* (Wiley, 2012), *Taming the Email Tiger* (Bacchus, 2008), and several other books, including a novel, a theatrical play, and the first published personal account of Hurricane Katrina.

Contributors

Lori J. Ashley In 2017 Lori Ashley joined Preservica, a digital preservation software provider, after 14 years as an independent records management consultant and educator dedicated to helping public and private sector organizations improve their record management and information governance practices. An experienced business strategist and organizational development specialist, Lori has a passion for developing approaches to foster collaboration among stakeholders who share accountability for effective and efficient lifecycle controls of valued records and information assets. In her current role as Preservica's Industry Market Development Manager, Lori analyzes industry and sector-specific business requirements to develop compelling use cases for digital preservation capabilities and solutions. Lori co-developed the Digital Preservation Capability Maturity Model (DPCMM) with Dr. Charles Dollar, and manages the www.DigitalOK.org self-assessment survey companion site.

Baird W. Brueseke, IGP, CIP, ECMp, CDIA, is a certified Information Governance Professional (IGP) with a focus on cyber-security issues. He has more than 25 years of experience leading companies and designing solutions to solve customer problems. He was inducted into AIIM's Company of Fellows in 2009. Early on, he designed several data collection systems for Children's Hospital in Los Angeles, including one of the first systems to use noninvasive measurements to automate the analysis of cardiovascular performance. He has headed a special consulting team, which automated EOB processing at Scripps Hospital, Patient Encounter (ICD9/CPT codes) at Sharp Healthcare, and HCFA forms processing solutions for medical billing processors.

Brueseke currently focuses on education and cyber-security. He is coauthor of the Virtual Instruction Cloud (Patent Application No: 13/939,139; pending). He also created a cloud-based portal, Computer Lab as a Service (ClaaS), which provides a hands-on computer laboratory experience to distance learners. Baird has performed Security Assessments and HIPAA compliance audits on hospitals, healthcare service providers, and regional Health Information Exchanges. For several years, he served on the HIMSS Cloud Security Working Group, serving as the liaison to the Cloud Security Alliance (CSA) and successfully advocating that HIMSS adopt the Cloud Security Controls embodied by the CSA's Cloud Controls Matrix (CCM) as their standard for Cloud Security instead of the proprietary HITRUST Controls.

Dr. Mansur Hasib, CISSP, PMP, CPHIMS 2017 Cybersecurity People's Choice Award and 2017 IG Expert of the Year Award winner, Dr. Hasib has 30 years' experience in leading organizational transformations through digital leadership and cyber-security strategy in healthcare, biotechnology, education, and energy. He has been a CIO, earned a Doctor of Science in Cybersecurity (IA), and the prestigious CISSP, PMP, and CPHIMS certifications. Dr. Hasib currently teaches graduate students and executives worldwide and is Program Chair of the (ISC)2 Americas ISLA

Award Winning Master of Science in Cybersecurity Technology Degree Program in The Graduate School at University of Maryland University College (UMUC).

He is the author of *Cyber-security Leadership: Powering the Modern Organization*, which received two nominations for The Cybersecurity Canon Hall of Fame. He conducted a national study of U.S. healthcare cyber-security and published the book *Impact of Security Culture on Security Compliance in Healthcare in the USA* (Tomorrow's Strategy Today, 2013).

Andrew Harvey, AMIRMS, is an ambitious and highly motivated health and social care professional with over 20 years' experience in the sector. He is a passionate IG and Data Protection/GDPR practitioner who, since 2005, has worked with a variety of healthcare information processes across the U.K.'s National Health Service (NHS) and independent/charity sector, including provider, shared business, and commissioning services.

He works with passion and enthusiasm to maintain the confidentiality, integrity, availability and accountability of patient and staff personal confidential data, as well as corporate information. Andrew thoroughly believes that when data is expertly managed, it improves the experience and quality of care that patients receive, while maintaining organizational professionalism and reputation.

He is an accredited member of the Information and Records Management Society and was nominated for its 2017 "Professional of the Year" Award.

Dennis Kessler is Head of Data Governance at the European Investment Bank. He is an information and change management professional with more years' experience than he is willing to admit. He has worked internationally on numerous initiatives for major organizations in the banking and health sectors, in addition to several years as a business writer and editor for the Economist Intelligence Unit during 10 years in Hong Kong and Osaka, Japan. After 10 years as a London-based consultant, Dennis spent five years at the Bank for International Settlements in Basel, Switzerland, including two years defining and establishing information governance, before relocating to Luxembourg with the European Investment Bank.

Richard P. Kessler is Director of Cyber Security Services Strategy and Governance at KPMG U.S. out of New York City. Previously, he was responsible for Information Lifecycle Governance at UBS, serving as the Risk Controller for records management, eDiscovery, and related disciplines. He managed the IG portfolio, defined and implemented control frameworks, developed and communicated business requirements and standards, and was the primary liaison to Compliance and Operational Risk for monitoring and assessing IG processes. For more than 25 years, Kessler has worked in numerous IT and Legal roles, including those in enterprise architecture, application development, trade automation, and data architecture. He has also served as an ESI/eDiscovery consultant, assisting law firms and corporations with litigation readiness and response strategies.

Reynold Leming is an experienced information governance professional and co-owner of Informu Solutions Ltd, a U.K.-based records management services and software company. Reynold is on the Executive Committee of the U.K.'s Information and Records Management Society. As a core offering, Informu develops and provides a dedicated information asset register software solution. Reynold has spent over 20 years in the document and records management industry, both working for leading vendors and then running his own business. Prior to this he worked in the city of London for 10 years, working for leading vendors of financial data and investment management software. Reynold is particularly interested in the legal aspects of information management, especially as applying to regulated and citizen-focused sectors such as the NHS, local government, and financial services.

Patricia Morris is a subject matter expert on records and information management with over 20 years of experience at several global pharmaceutical companies. As a strategic leader, her work has supported all areas of the business, with a focus on records and information in all formats (paper and electronic) generated during drug development. In her current role at eArchive Science, LLC, Patti delivers modern solutions for managing essential business records in any format through their entire lifespan to clients in the United States and EU. Her specialty areas include defining and delivering long-term digital preservation and electronic archiving solutions, developing and implementing records retention policies and schedules, as well as IG framework planning and execution.

Barry Moult is originally from Stoke on Trent, England, and started nurse training in the early 1970s and worked in Occupational Health through the 1980s. He moved to welfare work for the British Forces in the late 1980s and supplied IT Training for a private company and for Cardiff Prison. Barry continued to work as a nurse in A&E and with senior clinical duties. In 2000, he became the Data Protection Officer at West Suffolk Hospital. Barry founded and has chaired the Eastern Region IG Forum since 2003 and chairs the NHS National Information Governance Network Chairs group. Barry prefers "face-to-face" training to e-learning and is an advocate of IG Peer Review.

IG PROGRAM CONSIDERATIONS AND PLANNING

1

Chapter 1

The Healthcare Information Governance Imperative

I t could very well be that bad information is killing Americans at record rates. *Medical mistakes kill over 250,000 people each year in the U.S.*

It is the third leading cause of death overall, behind heart disease and cancer, according to a study by doctors at Johns Hopkins.[1] These numbers are certainly low, since they do not include deaths at nursing homes, surgery centers, and in-home care settings.

The United States has the most expensive healthcare in the world: the most advanced equipment, the most advanced medicines, the best-trained doctors—yet in a recent study of healthcare quality the U.S. came in dead last out of 11 civilized nations.[2] The U.K., Switzerland, and Sweden topped the list. Most Americans would be shocked to learn this.

The U.S. healthcare problem is not due to poor training, faulty equipment, inferior medicines, or lack of financial resources. No, the problem is likely primarily *a failure to get the right information to the right people at the right time*; that is, caregivers must have accurate, current clinical information to do their jobs properly.

This is an information governance (IG) issue that has life or death consequences. It can be fixed, but healthcare professionals must gain the necessary education and tools, collaborate with experts and each other, and gain executive management support for IG programs.

Across the pond, the issues facing the United Kingdom's government-funded National Health Service (NHS) are somewhat different, where IG has been an area of focus to ensure data quality and protect patient data for more than fifteen years. Although IG was mentioned in journals and scholarly articles decades ago, the U.K. is perhaps the home of healthcare IG, and arguably the IG discipline.[3] Could this be the reason the U.K. leads the world in healthcare quality? Certainly, it must be a major contributing factor.

Since 2002, each U.K. healthcare organization has been tasked with completing the IG Toolkit, managed by NHS Digital for the U.K. Department of Health. Although the IG Toolkit has evolved over the years, its core has remained constant. However, in April 2018 it was replaced with a new tool, the Data Security and Protection Toolkit, based around 10 National Data Security Standards that have been formulated by the U.K.'s National Data Guardian.[4]

3

At the same time the U.K. and the whole of the European Union is replacing its Data Protection legislation. In the U.K., the Data Protection Act 1998, itself based on a 1995 EU Data Protection Directive, is being replaced with the directly applicable (Brexit notwithstanding) EU **General Data Protection Regulation** (GDPR) and (at this writing) pending **Domestic Data Protection Act 2018**.

If U.K. healthcare IG professionals weren't busy enough keeping up with those major regulatory changes, the Care Quality Commission (U.K. regulator) has recently been given increased powers to inspect around IG issues, as a result of the global **WannaCry** ransomware attack in May 2017. So there is a massive push for healthcare organizations to implement a government-sponsored Cyber Essentials information security certification scheme.

These challenges for IG practitioners must be met within the construct of real-world needs, that is, to share ePHI more safely as the healthcare system attempts to create system-wide Sustainability and Transformation Plans/Accountable Care Organisations. As has been the case globally, securely sharing ePHI has been problematic so IG facets like privacy, data governance, and cyber-security have a prominent focus. Previous attempts in the last two decades to create a national U.K. network to share health information failed.[5]

U.S. Healthcare Organizations Ramping up IG Programs

According to a recent study, healthcare organizations in the U.S. are increasingly embarking on IG program implementations.[6] Although still in the early stages of adoption, organizations are beginning to understand that IG programs and a focus on clinical data quality is an important strategy for succeeding in today's competitive and increasingly digital healthcare business environment.

IG strategies also address the onslaught of data due to the Big Data trend, that is, a vast increase in the volume, variety, and velocity of data that is being created. Healthcare professionals clearly realize there are opportunities in applying advanced analytics to the mountains of data they are accumulating.

IG programs also address related information management and governance challenges such as the patient privacy, information security, regulatory compliance, **information lifecycle management** (ILM), and governing newer technologies like **the Internet of Things** (IoT).

Legal, regulatory, and information security demands are often key drivers for establishing IG programs in all industries, but in healthcare, information quality and control is paramount to improved patient care and outcomes.

Unforeseen Consequences in the Rush to Automate

The American Recovery and Reinvestment Act required that "all public and private healthcare providers and other eligible professionals (EP)" implement electronic health record (EHR) systems, and show *meaningful use* by January 1, 2014.[7] Meaningful use has a somewhat subjective definition, as stated by HealthIT.gov and other organizations. It means that EHR systems improve care coordination, quality, safety, efficiency, and "engage patients fully" while keeping their health information safe and private.[8] Industry estimates often peg meaningful use as utilizing about 40% of overall EHR system capabilities.

EHR automation was mandated by the federal government, and healthcare organizations were threatened with a decrease in Medicaid and Medicare reimbursement levels if they did not implement by the deadline. The result of the mandate to automate, and the mad rush to install EHR systems and to prove meaningful use resulted in many sloppy, haphazard implementations. What is mostly missing are redesigned business processes with a built-in focus on not only data quality and governance but also information privacy and security. Further, the ability to share information between disparate EHR systems to provide continuity of care is generally lacking.[9]

A focus on data quality, from the ground up, means that clinical assumptions and insights are more accurate, and subsequent downstream reports and analyses are more accurate and trusted. Unfortunately, the consequences in the healthcare environment are much more dire compared to other industries: Bad information means people could die.

The consequences of this general carelessness with information in the healthcare industry have resulted in colossal IG failures that almost daily expose major organizations to reputational and financial risk. For instance, in 2018, **LifeBridge Health** revealed that the electronic health records (EHR) of over 500,000 patients had been compromised, for over a year.[10] In 2017, major breaches included the **Molina Healthcare** breach, which may have compromised 4.8 million patient records, and at **Mid-Michigan Physicians Imaging Center** potentially over 100,000 patients' ePHI was breached. The Center delayed reporting the breach while they investigated, and ended up paying a $475,000 fine levied by the Health and Human Services' Office of Civil Rights (OCR). The **21st Century Oncology** breach in 2015 exposed 2,213,597 patients' records.[11] 21st Century Oncology was fined $2.3 million by the OCR. And in 2015, major breaches included **Premera BlueCross, Excellus BlueCross BlueShield**,[12] and **Anthem Health**, where rogue hackers penetrated the organization and stole possibly over 37.5 million records.[13] These organizations obviously did not know where all their protected health information (PHI), personally identifiable information (PII), and confidential electronic documents were located and took inadequate measures to secure that valuable information.

They—and most healthcare organizations—are not managing information as an asset, are not assessing its risks, and do not have a current inventory or accounting of their information assets, particularly sensitive or confidential information. That is, there is no **data map** showing where different types of information are stored, and most organizations would have difficulty finding all incidences of it so that confidential and sensitive information may be secured.

Most organizations are not paying attention: they leave ePHI and sensitive information (such as race, religion, and ethnicity) out there floating around on their servers unsecured, unencrypted. When it comes time to attend to the problem, most often they "kick the can down the road" and do nothing, since it costs time and money to address the issue. Executives perhaps have their eye on year-end bonuses, not lingering risks. But eventually risks can come home to roost, with horrendous consequences.

The impact only becomes clear after a major event like a data breach or ransomware attack. These types of IG failures can severely damage an organization's reputation—especially healthcare institutions where people's health and lives are at stake—and can result in injury, death, and financial loss. Also, thousands of patients can be dragged into a lifelong battle to control their personal information and ePHI.

Ransomware is a major problem. When rogue hackers use ransomware techniques, they take control of an organization's information and will not release it until a ransom is paid.

When surveyed, nearly 70% of U.S. consumers said they would consider leaving their healthcare provider if it suffered a ransomware attack.[14]

Consumers have higher expectations of healthcare providers to keep their data safe, versus other industries, like retailers. Consumers hold healthcare organizations responsible for the security and privacy of their information, not information security software providers or even the government.

There are some basic truths about information security, and one of them is: *perimeter security of most networks is easily breached.* So sensitive and confidential information must be identified, secured, tracked, and controlled. That means locking down ePHI and ePII with encryption or related technologies.

And when the organization has finished utilizing personal information, it must be discarded according to most state privacy laws, yet medical records must be maintained to facilitate continuity and lifelong care (most U.S. states recommend seven years retention beyond the last care episode, whereas the California Hospital Association recommends 10 years).[15] These conflicting demands make information lifecycle management more complicated for healthcare organizations.

These complex and sometimes competing demands on information assets mean an IG program must be in place with the formal policies and procedures necessary to govern them. IG programs also help organizations meet compliance and legal demands while improving quality clinical and financial information provided to caregivers and managers for decision-making. Its win-win-win all around, but it is also a major undertaking that requires an executive management commitment to a long-term, "evergreen" IG program.

Major IG Failures

Here are three examples of IG failures, which were very public. These instances bring IG weaknesses fully into view, and demonstrate the critical need for IG programs in healthcare organizations.

Case Brief #1: Associates in Psychiatry and Psychology Ransomware Attack: A Model Response?

Ransomware attacks are among the most serious and prevalent threats for data, especially in the healthcare sector. Ransomware is best understood as a type of malicious software that intends to either publish or block access to information until a "ransom" is paid. While ransomware attacks have increased in complexity, and the ability to reverse them along with it, encrypting files and making them inaccessible until the ransom payment provides real problems for organizations that store massive amounts of personal data.

One of the latest attacks, on the Rochester (Minnesota)–based Associates in Psychiatry and Psychology (APP),[16] was revealed on March 31, 2018. The ransomware attack affected patient information for 6,546 individuals; it appeared that the information was not in a "human-readable" format and that the protected health information wasn't accessed or copied by the attackers.

Ransomware attacks like this speak to the need for information governance and privacy protection programs.

APP had a prompt response to the attack, taking their systems offline. Doing so in a timely manner likely stopped the spread of the attack and limited possible encryption of personal data and data theft, completing the "ransom" aspect of the ransomware attack.

APP, in a Q&A regarding the incident, reported that it was a "Triple-M" ransomware attack. This variation uses the RSA-2048 encryption protocol, which utilizes long keys in order to encrypt the data. A ransom was paid, as the backups with the restore files could not be accessed based on the attack. The initial ransom demand of 4 Bitcoin ($30,000) was not paid and instead negotiated down to .5 BTC ($3,800). With the systems and data now restored, APP has installed additional layers of security as well as new remote access policies.

Ransomware attacks are not unique, even within the healthcare sector. What is fascinating about this attack is the amount of information shared with affected patients and the openness with which APP talked about the breach. Most breaches go unnoticed in the public eye because very little information is shared with the general public, even those directly affected, especially if the data wasn't accessed or copied. APP's transparency provides affected parties the ability to understand how the breach affects them and what they can do to protect themselves.

Other organizations should stand up and take note: APP's response should become the standard.

Case Brief #2: An Information Governance Failure: Anthem, Inc.

In 2016, a year after the largest healthcare data breach to date, where as many as 40 million confidential records of members and employees at Anthem, Inc., were hacked, little had been learned about the nature, motivations, implications, and real costs of the breach.[17] According to Anthem the data breach affected several of its brands, including Anthem Blue Cross, Anthem Blue Cross and Blue Shield, Blue Cross and Blue Shield of Georgia, Empire Blue Cross and Blue Shield, Amerigroup, Caremore, and UniCare.

Anthem, the nation's second largest health insurer, had insurance themselves—cyber-insurance. Perhaps that was why executives felt assured prior to the attack. Most of the initial costs were likely absorbed by a $100 million AIG cyber-insurance policy. But there have been many class action lawsuits filed, and "unresolved legal issues likely have stifled further disclosure of what is known."[18]

By law, Anthem was not required to encrypt the PII, although this is a standard industry best practice. Certainly, victims sued Anthem just on the basis that they did not take proper care of their PII while in their custody.

The PII compromised included, names, addresses, birthdates, social security numbers, medical IDs, e-mail addresses and salary and employment information.[19] Anthem provided two years of credit monitoring for those who were affected. This was a mild measure, as hackers usually wait years to sell compromised data.

Certainly, Anthem's reputation was damaged, and the massive breach led to acquisition target Cigna questioning Anthem's information governance posture, data privacy, and security measures, and the resultant legal impact. In a letter, Cigna's CEO and former Board Chairman wrote, "Trust with customers and providers is critical in our industry, and Anthem has yet to demonstrate a path toward restoring this trust. We need to understand the litigation and potential liabilities, operational impact and long-term damage to Anthem's franchise as a result of this unprecedented data breach, as well as the governance and controls that resulted in this system failure."[20]

But a year after the event—since the lawsuits had not been settled—there had been no significant impact on Anthem's profits. Anthem executives essentially buried the breach event, as they did not address it and its impact on their quarterly earnings calls in the year after the breach.

So far, according to the FBI, there has been no evidence that the compromised records have been sold—*although a common tactic of hackers is to wait until the breach has been forgotten before they attempt to sell the data.*

Anthem has taken steps to shore up its information security practices, hiring cyber-security firm Mandiant just after the attack. Also the National Association of Insurance Commissioners (NAIC) commissioned a "market conduct and financial exam" of the breach, but the report is classified.

Case Brief #3: 21st Century Oncology

In late 2015, hackers compromised the records of approximately 2.2 million current and former patients of 21st Century Oncology, the largest radiation oncology provider in the U.S., which operates nearly 200 cancer treatment centers in the U.S. and Latin America.[21] In 2017, 21st Century Oncology declared bankruptcy and paid a $2.3 million fine to the U.S. Department of Health and Human Services.[22]

Patients were notified that their PII and PHI had been compromised, including names, social security numbers, physician names, diagnoses, treatment course, and insurance information.

Health information is the most valuable to hackers, more valuable than credit card information, which can be changed and nullified quickly and has liability limits. Stolen health credentials do not have an expiration date, and can fetch up to 50 times the value of credit card identity information. Forged or fake healthcare insurance credentials can allow rogue patients to undergo surgeries and expensive treatments and bill them to the identity theft victim's insurance, possibly leaving them with a large co-pay bill. Expensive procedures like hip replacements and even heart surgery have been performed on patients using stolen medical credentials.

Between 15 and 20 separate class action lawsuits were filed against 21st Century Oncology as a result of the breach. A U.S. magistrate judge recommended the consolidation of the cases into a single class-action claim. Victims of the breach have reported various incidents where they have already been impacted, such as unauthorized closing of bank accounts, and harassing and fraudulent phone calls, including some where criminals pose as IRS agents attempting to collect taxes that were not owed.

Other victims are legally pursuing the handling of the breach incident response, since 21st Century Oncology waited more than three months after the FBI notified them to notify those affected. Company officials cited the criminal investigation as the reason for the delay.

21st Century Oncology did provide one year of identity fraud protection to those whose records were compromised. *One of the victims was not able to sign up, as someone had already used her credentials to do so!*

A large number of victims notified about the breach had no knowledge they might be affected, since the healthcare facility they used operated under another brand name.

The 21st Century Oncology data breach demonstrates that most organizations are ill-prepared to prevent or respond to a major data breach. They have not done regular cyber-security vulnerability assessments or live penetration tests to find where their weaknesses are, before rogue players do. They have not invested enough in privacy measures and breach response protocols. IG programs address these key issues on a consistent, methodical basis and reduce the likelihood that the major breaches will occur, and if they do, lessen their impact.

Information Assurance: Trusted and Accurate Information

With accurate and trusted information, healthcare professionals can do the job they were trained to do, and drastically reduce medical mistakes. This is an IG effort with the highest purpose: one that will save lives.

On top of this noble pursuit to save lives by improving information and its delivery are the layers upon layers of regulatory compliance requirements, and increased litigation demands, all of which add cost to healthcare operations. These forces are adding increased cost pressures to U.S. healthcare organizations, which are already under pressure to cut costs and perform financially.

On the positive, side, IG efforts in healthcare have the opportunity to greatly improve clinical insights by leveraging advanced analytics. This has the potential to improve healing, recovery rates, and patient satisfaction. Further, financial and service innovations can arise from new insights gained by leveraging business analytics and other tools.

Healthcare, particularly in the U.S., is at a crisis point, having invested so much in automation, training, and advanced equipment and medicines—yet yielding such troubling results in healthcare quality and outcomes. The move to value-based care approaches will help address this issue, along with increased IG adoption.

Strong, ongoing IG programs can help harness the power of all the investments in clinical and financial systems that have been made, and improve results for patients and other healthcare stakeholders.

Chapter Summary: Key Points

- **Poor Information Governance (IG) and data quality practices may largely be the cause of over 250,000 people dying of medical mistakes each year in the U.S.**
- The practice of IG in healthcare began in the U.K. in 2002.
- Major regulatory changes in the U.K. and Europe are forcing IG programs into greater prominence and maturity.
- Medical mistakes are the third leading cause of death in the U.S.
- The U.S. has the most expensive healthcare in the world, yet it is rated poorly in healthcare quality when compared to other civilized nations.
- With accurate and trusted information, healthcare professionals can do the job they were trained to do, and drastically reduce medical mistakes.
- The U.S. government mandate to automate and install electronic health record (EHR) systems over the past several years has resulted in a lot of sloppy, haphazard implementations.
- Healthcare organizations are starting to implement IG programs in the U.S. and are beginning to understand that IG is an important strategy to meet pressing information demands.
- Business processes must be redesigned with a built-in focus on information privacy and security and also data governance and quality. These are IG program efforts.
- IG addresses issues such as data quality and integrity, lifecycle information management, patient privacy, and compliance. Legal, regulatory, and information security concerns also are drivers for establishing an IG program.

Notes

1. Jen Christensen and Elizabeth Cohen, "Medical Errors May Be Third Leading Cause of Death in the U.S.," CNN.com, May 4, 2016, http://edition.cnn.com/2016/05/03/health/medical-error-a-leading-cause-of-death.

2. Dan Munro, "U.S. Healthcare Ranked Dead Last Compared to 10 Other Countries," Forbes, June 16, 2014, http://www.forbes.com/sites/danmunro/2014/06/16/u-s-healthcare-ranked-dead-last-compared-to-10-other-countries/#7aa717021b96.

3. Andrew Harvey and Barry Moult, e-mail to author February 25, 2018.

4. Ibid.

5. Ibid.

6. "Information Governance in Healthcare: A Call to Adopt Information Governance Practices," AHIMA and Cohassett Associates, 2014, p. 12, http://research.zarca.com/Survey.aspx?k=SsURPPsUSVsPsPsP&Lang=0&Status=&Data=&Dir=NXT&Uid=802346543&rnd2=1&rnd=7771.698151106978.

7. "Federal Mandates for Healthcare: Digital Record-Keeping Requirements for Public and Private Healthcare Providers," USF Health Online, https://www.usfhealthonline.com/resources/healthcare/electronic-medical-records-mandate.

8. Ibid.

9. Vicki Skidmore, RHIS, IGP, e-mail to author March 1, 2018.

10. Beth Jones Sanborn, "LifeBridge Health Reveals Breach That Compromised Health Data of 500,000 Patients," Healthcare IT News, May 23, 2018, https://www.healthcareitnews.com/news/lifebridge-health-reveals-breach-compromised-health-data-500000-patients.

11. "Major 2016 Healthcare Data Breaches: Mid Year Summary," HIPAA Journal, July 11, 2016, http://www.hipaajournal.com/major-2016-healthcare-data-breaches-mid-year-summary-3499.

12. Jessica Davis, "7 Largest Data Breaches of 2015," Healthcare IT News, December 11, 2015, http://www.healthcareitnews.com/news/7-largest-data-breaches-2015.

13. Cameron F. Kerry, "Lessons from the New Threat Environment from Sony, Anthem and ISIS," Brookings Institution, March 26, 2015, http://www.brookings.edu/blogs/techtank/posts/2015/03/26-anthem-sony-isis-hack-cybersecurity.

14. Rebecca Wynn, CISSP, CRISC, CASP, CCISO, LinkedIn post, May 31, 2017.

15. Vicki Skidmore, RHIS, IGP, e-mail to author March 1, 2018.

16. Jessica Davis, "Minnesota Ransomware Attack Shows the Right Way to Handle Breach Response," Healthcare IT News, May 25, 2018, https://www.healthcareitnews.com/news/minnesota-ransomware-attack-shows-right-way-handle-breach-response.

17. Bob Herman, "Details of Anthem's Massive Cyberattack Remain in the Dark a Year later," Modern Healthcare, March 30, 2016, http://www.modernhealthcare.com/article/20160330/NEWS/160339997.

18. Ibid.

19. "Anthem Medical Data Breach," Wikipedia.org, last modified November 20, 2017, https://en.wikipedia.org/wiki/Anthem_medical_data_breach.

20. Herman, "Details of Anthem's Massive Cyberattack."

21. Frank Gluck, "21st Century Oncology Data Breach Prompts Multiple Lawsuits," News-Press, July 22, 2016, http://www.news-press.com/story/news/2016/07/22/21st-century-oncology-data-breach-prompts-multiple-lawsuits/87386068.

22. Jessica Davis, "21st Century Oncology to Pay OCR $2.3 Million for 2015 Breach," Healthcare IT News, December 13, 2017, http://www.healthcareitnews.com/news/21st-century-oncology-pay-ocr-23-million-2015-breach.

Chapter 2

Information Governance: Key Concepts and Definitions

Many healthcare professionals are somewhat confused about the definition of **information governance** (IG). IG has suffered through dozens of definitions, some that are incorrect and some fabulously verbose, causing IG to become a foggy and often misunderstood concept.

This chapter will simplify the definitions, concepts, and core strategies so that they are clear and actionable for healthcare professionals.

According to the Sedona Conference, information governance is about *minimizing information risks and costs and maximizing information value.*[1] This is a compact way to convey the key aims of IG programs, and it is what should be emphasized when the merits of an IG program are discussed.

The definition of IG can be distilled further. An even more succinct "elevator pitch" definition of IG is, *"security, control, and optimization"* of information.

This is a short definition that anyone can remember. It is a useful one for communicating the basics of IG to executives.

To go into more detail: This definition means that information—particularly confidential, personal, or other sensitive information—is kept **secure** in its three states: at rest, in transit, and also (the most difficult), in use.

It means that your organizational IG processes **control** *who* has access to *which* information, and *when.* That means the right information is available to the right people, at the right time.

And it means that information that no longer has business value is destroyed and the most valuable information is leveraged to provide new insights and value. In other words, it is **optimized.**

What all the presented definitions are getting at is what it means to *govern* information, as opposed to leaving it uncontrolled and unprotected, and allowing it to spiral out of control, exposing the organization to undue risks.

A more detailed definition from the American Health Information Management Association (AHIMA) states that IG is *"an organization-wide framework for managing information throughout its lifecycle and supporting the organization's strategy, operations, regulatory, legal, risk, and environmental requirements."*[2]

To delve more deeply into this definition, it is useful to examine key phrases it contains:[3]

Organization-wide. IG programs are necessarily cross-functional, involving multiple functions of the organization working together in a collaborative way. Key stakeholders include Information Technology (IT), Legal, Health Information Management (HIM) and business Records Management (RM), Patient Privacy, Information Security, Risk Management, Compliance, and more, depending on the goals and focus of the IG program. IG programs seek to break down functional silos and to foster a collaborative view of information, where its risks and value are considered from a broader viewpoint across organizational functions. The idea is that information has greater value when it is shared and leveraged as an asset across the organization—perhaps re-purposed or re-packaged—and through tools like analytics, new insights, strategies, and innovations may emerge. Also, taking an organization-wide view of key IG facets like information risk and cyber-security will facilitate the development of a broader and more effective information security program. For instance, as a part of an overall IG program, security awareness training (SAT) can be conducted on an ongoing basis, educating not only the IT department but all employees on new threats, phishing schemes, and ransomware attacks;

Framework. An **Information Governance framework** (IGF) is required to serve as the "guardrails" for your IG program. Each IG framework will look a little different but there are commonalities that appear in successful ones.[4] Some key components of an IG Framework that will serve as the construct, the foundation for your successful IG program include:

1. *Business Objectives* – A focus delivering value and assisting the organization in meeting its key business objectives;
2. *Executive Sponsor* – Must be high level, committed to the long term, and have a vested interest in the success of the IG program by developing the business case for it. Also, it is advisable to have a deputy sponsor to ensure the continuity of the program long term, improving its durability;
3. *IG Lead* – The person responsible for the day-to-day management of the IG program. They could come from a business analyst background, IT, Cyber-security, Risk Management, HIM, Legal, or Operations, but most of all this person must be a great communicator and collaborator;
4. *Cross-Functional IG Steering Committee* – Made up of department heads or leaders from Legal, IT, HIM and RM, Privacy, Security, Finance, and perhaps others such as Risk Management, Human Resources (HR), Analytics, and other business units, depending on the focus and charter of the IG program;
5. *Program Charter* – This written document spells out the purpose or mission, business objectives, scope, team member responsibilities, meeting frequency, and other program attributes. It must be signed off on by the executive sponsor;
6. *An Evaluation of External Business, Legal, and Economic Factors* – Considering the present and projected regulatory environment, business and competitive environment, technology advancements, litigation profile/legal scenario, and other external factors;
7. *IG Maturity Models* – These should be leveraged in the IG effort, and there are various models to suit different assessment goals. A broad, encompassing, and detailed model that measures maturity on 22 IG-related processes is **the IG Process Maturity Model** (IGPMM) from the Compliance, Governance, and Oversight Council (CGOC).[5] The IGPMM was developed in 2012, and updated in 2017 to include considerations for cloud computing, cyber-security, privacy, and more. It is a comprehensive model applicable to all industries, which emphasizes privacy, security, and legal processes. For healthcare

specifically, the newer (and less mature) IG Adoption Model™ from AHIMA measures maturity of 10 organizational "competencies" which AHIMA states are tied directly to Merit-based Incentive Payment System (MIPS) performance categories and help organizations improve performance under the Medicare Access and CHIP Reauthorization Act (MACRA).[6] When looking at component IG areas, there are other maturity models to consider. For example, for analytics functions, the HIMSS Analytics Adoption Model for Analytics Maturity (AMAM); for e-health records, the HIMSS Maturity Model for Electronic Medical Record (MMEMR) and the Continuity of Care Maturity Model CCMM), and also the Electronic Patient Record Maturity Model (EPRMM) for systems that manage all patient information.[7]

8. *Standards* – It may be helpful to use certain standards to help guide IG program efforts, such as ISO 9000 quality guidelines for healthcare,[8] ISO 31000 for risk management, ISO 27001/2 for information security, ISO 38500 for IT governance, ISO 22301 for business continuity, and other standards that may be relevant to the IG program focus and can help guide efforts;

9. *Program Communications & Training* – The IG program must include a communications and training component as a standard function. Get creative. Make it fun. Use posters, create a slogan, have contests or gamify training. Maybe even create a mascot. Engaged learners absorb and retain much more. Your stakeholder audience must be made aware of new policies and practices that are to be followed, and how this new approach contributes toward accomplishing business objectives. But critically, *they must receive training on the new approach,* as well as constant and consistent reinforcement of new IG precepts;

10. *Program Metrics, Monitoring, Auditing & Enforcement* – How do you know how well you are doing? Between major maturity model assessments, continual feedback is needed to adjust and fine-tune the IG program. The program must have established metrics and controls to determine the level of employee conformance, its impact on key operational areas, and progress made toward key business objectives. Parts of the program can be made fun, gamified, to keep stakeholders engaged. For instance, watching a security awareness training (SAT) video and completing a quiz on the day it is released, could be worth more points than completing the assignment in 2–3 days. Testing and auditing provide an opportunity to give feedback to employees on how well they are doing and to recommend changes they may make. And having objective feedback on key metrics also will allow your executive sponsor to see where progress has been made, and where improvements need to focus.

By including the above elements in your IG Framework your organization will have established a solid foundation to build your IG program, and it will have greatly increased its odds of success. An IGF needs to be modified according to the competitive scenario, external business environment, and available resources (e.g. human resources, skillsets, budget). (*More detail will be provided on building your IGF later in this book.*)

Lifecycle. Managing the lifecycle of information properly and securely from creation, though use, to storage and archiving, and even planned and proven destruction (disposition) at the end of its lifecycle.

Organization's strategy. IG strategy must align with overall organizational strategy to support the accomplishment of business objectives. An IG program can assist in improving data quality and patient care, reducing information risks and costs, reducing legal expenses and even possibly increasing revenues, while improving operational efficiency.

IG Programs Must Become Embedded

For IG programs to deliver consistent, long-term benefits, they must become as embedded as a workplace safety program. They must constantly be reinforced, updated, expanded, and promoted. IG programs require a significant **change management** effort to educate departments on the goals and objectives of the program, and to "sell" individuals on the validity and benefits of the IG program effort.

IG Programs Are about Enforcing Policy Consistently

Standardized and systematized IG policy means that information assets are identified (mapped) and **classified**, and, if justified, protected with security technologies like **encryption**.

IG also means that all copies of health records and **vital records**—those which the organization absolutely must have to continue operations in the event of a disaster—are located, classified, and safeguarded properly. This requires a records inventory and creation of a data map.

Practicing good IG means managing the information lifecycle: that information is kept as long as required by regulations and statutes, and internal business needs, and then it is discarded according to an established retention and disposition schedule (unless it is subject to a legal hold during litigation or other regulatory requirements). Think of it as getting rid of information that no longer has value to make room for new, high-value information.

When information asset stores are kept cleaned up, there are ongoing benefits. Not just lower operating costs and improved productivity, but also the information that remains has higher value to the business and can be leveraged using advanced analytics to create new insights that feed into management decisions. This can provide a sustainable strategic advantage.

The Key Differences between Data Governance and Information Governance

Data governance (DG) and information governance (IG) are often confused.

They are distinct disciplines, but DG is a subset of IG, and should be a part of an overall IG program. DG is the most rudimentary level to implement IG, and often DG programs provide the springboard for IG programs.

Data Governance expert Bob Seiner, author of *The Data Administration Newsletter* for over 20 years, who pioneered the concept of "non-invasive data governance" offers his definition of data governance, "Data governance is the execution and enforcement of authority over the definition, production and usage of data." He goes on to say, "My definition intentionally has some grit and some teeth—I fully stand behind having strong definition especially if it catches people's attention and opens the door for greater discussion. At the end of the day, true governance over data or information requires executed and enforced authority."

Data governance entails maintaining clean, unique (nonduplicate), structured data (in databases). Structured data is typically about 10%–20% of the total amount of information stored in an organization, but this ratio is higher in healthcare organizations due to the volumes of clinical data.

Often, a formal Chief Data Officer (CDO) who deals with data quality, privacy, security, analytics, and governance oversees data governance.

DG includes data modeling and data security, and also utilizes data cleansing (or data scrubbing) to strip out corrupted, inaccurate, or extraneous data, as well as de-duplication to eliminate redundant occurrences of data. Data governance focuses on *data quality* from the ground up at the lowest or root level, so that subsequent clinical assessments, reports, analyses, and conclusions are based on clean, reliable, trusted data in database tables. *This is especially critical when dealing with clinical data.*

The Challenge: Managing Unstructured Information

Unstructured information is the vast majority of information that healthcare organizations struggle to manage. Unstructured information includes radiologic and scanned images, progress notes, audio recordings of patient consultations, video files, e-mail messages, word processing documents, PDF documents, presentation slides, spreadsheets, and the like.

Unstructured information is more challenging to manage than structured information in databases and is the primary focus of many IG programs. Unstructured or semi-structured information generally lacks detailed and consistent metadata to describe its contents. Methodically adding metadata to unstructured information helps an organization to categorize and manage it. There are software tools to assist in this effort, such **as file analysis classification and remediation** (FACR) software.

IG is much more broad and far-reaching than DG. IG is the overarching polices and processes to optimize and leverage information as an asset while keeping it secure and meeting legal and privacy obligations. These IG program aims should always be in alignment with stated organizational business objectives.

IG Requires Cross-Functional Collaboration

IG is a new, maturing discipline that most healthcare organizations have not yet begun to tackle due mostly to its complexity, vagueness, and cross-functional nature. Also, it typically is a challenging program to sell to senior management, due to its costs, often unclear initial benefits, long-term commitment, and many moving parts. Plus there are political issues. It involves coordination between IT, HIM, Information Security, Patient Privacy, Legal and Litigation Issues, Risk Management, business Records Management functions, and more. It is a complex amalgamated discipline, made up of multiple sub-disciplines.

IG must be driven from the top down by a strong executive sponsor, with day-to-day management by an IG Lead, which is a person who could come from one of the major sub-disciplines of IG. The IG Lead could come from HIM, IT, Cyber-security, Patient Privacy, Analytics, Legal, Operations, or related disciplines. The IG Lead must be well-versed in all of these disciplines to be most effective, although their role is mostly one of orchestrating or coaching the IG steering committee since typically the IG Lead does not have formal authority. More and more, however, a formal "Chief IG Officer" title is being given to the IG Lead.

IG programs across industries are often aimed at reducing legal costs and information risk. In healthcare, reducing medical mistakes and guarding patient privacy are major goals. These are big targets. However, the payoff can be huge, not only in cost reduction but in reducing information (and reputational) risk. Consider the cases of poor IG at Premera BlueCross, Excellus BlueCross BlueShield, or Anthem.

But the greatest benefits from IG programs will come when healthcare organizations value information as an asset, holistically, and are able to harvest valuable metadata and run analytics to gain new clinical and financial insights. This can improve patient outcomes, improve the patient experience, and help the organization to develop new services that help to maintain a competitive advantage.

The Facets of Information Governance

The components of IG are coming into clearer focus as the discipline matures. IG professionals were surveyed, and the results show a market that is maturing and coming into focus.

Consensus has been building as to IG's identity, and the market is solidifying. The key facets or functional areas of IG, according to one major survey, are:[9]

1. Records and Information Management (RIM/HIM)
2. Information Security
3. Compliance
4. E-discovery
5. Data governance
6. Privacy
7. Risk management
8. Data storage and archiving

Yet this finding may be skewed, based on the makeup of the polled group, perhaps heavily populated by records managers. The survey did not state the number, job description/category, or demographics of the polled group.

An IG maturity model with a research-based focus, the CGOC **Information Governance Process Maturity Model (IGPMM)**,[10] is based on the input of over 3,600 Legal, IT, and RIM professionals, and was updated in 2017.

In the IGPMM, *RIM constitutes only one of the 22 processes that are measured for IG program maturity*, whereas there are seven IT processes, six Legal/E-discovery processes, and four for Privacy and Security. This model may also have some bias; IBM is a founding sponsor of the CGOC and certainly is positioned mostly in the IT space.

This author believes that, based on industry trends and Best Practices, the importance of Privacy and Security roles in IG continue to increase and are generally of more significance to IG programs than IT everyday processes such as System Provisioning.

It is readily apparent just how far-reaching IG programs are—spanning a variety of functional groups. This is what makes IG efforts so challenging: they require collaboration across these various groups, which will have varying agendas, as well as individual personalities competing for advancement in the organization.

It is the executive sponsor's job to get the IG team to focus on business objectives which will benefit the organization as a whole. The IG Lead must execute the IG Strategic Plan which details the stated business goals and objectives; within the guardrails of the IG Framework; and in accordance with the IG Program Charter.

Forming sub-committees and focusing on discrete IG-related projects within your overall IG program can deliver near-term benefits that the executive sponsor can track. It will be clear that progress is being made. It will help to maintain focus and allow your organization to move forward, accruing the benefits of IG. Examples of short-term discrete projects that deliver almost immediate benefits include:

1. HIM Awareness Training
2. Information Security Awareness Training
3. Patient Privacy Awareness Training
4. Shared drive cleanup and remediation

5. Updating the Records Retention Schedule (RRS)
6. Updating departmental file plans
7. E-discovery Readiness Improvement
8. Legal Hold Notification (LHN) training and process improvement.

Getting some of these "quick wins" will provide momentum for the IG program and keep executives apprised of concrete progress.

Chapter Summary: Key Points

- **IG is about minimizing information risks and costs while maximizing its value.**
- IG is, in short, "security, control, & optimization of information."
- AHIMA defines IG as "an organization-wide framework for managing information throughout its lifecycle and supporting the organization's strategy, operations, regulatory, legal, risk, and environmental requirements."
- For IG programs to deliver consistent, long-term benefits, they must become as embedded as a workplace safety program.
- Data governance (DG) focuses on getting clean (structured) data into databases and leveraging it for improving patient outcomes and other business benefits. DG and can be considered a subset of IG, and often is a springboard for IG programs.
- Perimeter security of most networks is easily breached. So sensitive and confidential information, including PHI/PII and financial information, must be identified, secured, tracked, and controlled.
- IG means managing the information lifecycle.
- IG programs are necessarily cross-functional in nature. Key groups that must be involved include HIM, IT, Legal, Patient Privacy, Information Security, and possibly Risk Management, Analytics, and others, depending on the IG program focus.
- IG must be driven from the top down by a strong executive sponsor.
- Key facets of IG include: RIM and HIM, Information Security, Compliance, E-discovery, Data Governance, Patient Privacy, and Risk Management. Information security and privacy plays an increasing role in IG programs.

Notes

1. "Commentary on Information Governance," *The Sedona Conference Journal*, vol. xv (Fall 2014): 134, https://thesedonaconference.org/publications retrieved October 11, 2017.
2. Sofia Empel, "Way Forward: AHIMA Develops Information Governance Principles to Lead Healthcare Toward Better Data Management," *Journal of AHIMA* 85, no. 10 (October 2014): 30–32, http://library.ahima.org/doc?oid=107468#.Wd6MAMZryM8.
3. Ann Meehan, RHIA, "Information Governance—Are You Onboard?", *Journal of AHIMA* blog post, September 23, 2016, http://journal.ahima.org/2016/09/23/information-governance-are-you-onboard/.
4. Robert F. Smallwood, MBA, CIP, IGP, "Constructing Your Information Governance Framework," LinkedIn.com, June 12, 2015, https://www.linkedin.com/pulse/constructing-your-information-governance-framework-smallwood?trk=mp-reader-card.
5. "Latest CGOC Information Governance Process Maturity Model," CGOC, https://www.cgoc.com/updated-ig-process-maturity-model-reflects-todays-data-realities-2.

6. Kathy Downing, "Preparing for MACRA with AHIMA's Information Governance Adoption Model," *Journal of AHIMA* 89, no. 2 (February 2018): 28–29, http://www.ahimajournal-digital.com/ahimajournal/february_2018?pg=25#pg25.

7. João Vidal Carvalho, Álvaro Rocha, and António Abreu, "Maturity Models of Healthcare Information Systems and Technologies: A Literature Review," *Journal of Medical Systems* 40 (2016): 131, https://doi.org/10.1007/s10916-016-0486-5.

8. "ISO 9000 Guidelines for Health Care Sector," International Organization for Standardization, https://www.iso.org/news/2001/10/Ref802.html.

9. IG Initiative, 2015–16 State of the IG Industry Report, and 2017–18 State of the Industry Report, https://iginitiative.com/tag/2016-2017-igi-annual-survey/.

10. "Latest CGOC Information Governance Process Maturity Model," CGOC, https://www.cgoc.com/updated-ig-process-maturity-model-reflects-todays-data-realities-2/.

Chapter 3

Information Governance Principles

Using guiding principles to drive your information governance (IG) program can help educate stakeholders, focus efforts, and maintain consistency.

The Sedona Conference® Commentary on Information Governance

The Sedona Conference® is a group of mostly legal and technology professionals that meets periodically and develops commentary and guidance on e-discovery, electronic records, IG, and related issues. They have developed 11 general principles of IG,[1] which provide guidance on the expectations and aims of IG programs. These principles can further an IG team's understanding of IG and can be used from an introductory "IG Awareness Training" session to the early stages of your program launch. A good exercise is to have team members re-write these principles in their own words, and then hold discussions about how each of these principles would apply to their departmental IG efforts, and the overall IG program:

1. Organizations should consider implementing an IG program to make coordinated decisions about information for the benefit of the overall organization that address information-related requirements and manage risks while optimizing value.
2. An IG program should maintain sufficient independence from any particular department or division to ensure that decisions are made for the benefit of the overall organization.
3. All information stakeholders should participate in the IG program.
4. The strategic objectives of the IG program should be based upon a comprehensive assessment of information-related practices, requirements, risks, and opportunities.
5. An IG program should be established with the structure, direction, resources, and accountability to provide reasonable assurance that the program's objectives will be achieved.
6. The effective, timely, and consistent disposal of physical and electronic information that no longer needs to be retained should be a core component of any IG program.

7. When IG decisions require an organization to reconcile conflicting laws or obligations, the organization should act in good faith and give due respect to considerations such as privacy, data protection, security, records and information management, risk management, and sound business practices.

8. If an organization has acted in good faith in its attempt to reconcile conflicting laws and obligations, a court or other authority reviewing the organization's actions should do so under a standard of reasonableness according to the circumstances at the time such actions were taken.

9. An organization should consider reasonable measures to maintain the integrity and availability of long-term information assets throughout their intended useful life.

10. An organization should consider leveraging the power of new technologies in its IG program.

11. An organization should periodically review and update its IG program to ensure that it continues to meet the organization's needs as they evolve.

Smallwood IG Principles Applied to Healthcare Organizations

The following 10 IG Principles are the result of the author's research and consulting efforts over the past decade, where a great deal of practical information on IG program successes, failures, and Best Practices was synthesized, analyzed, and distilled.

These 10 IG principles must be adhered to as general guidelines for IG programs to succeed:

1. **Value information as an asset**. Just as any healthcare organization has physical assets like buildings, lab and diagnostic equipment, computers, software, and patient beds, etc., which have value, information collected and analyzed also has value. The formal management of information assets with the goal of monetizing and leveraging that information is clearly outlined in the book, *Infonomics: How to Monetize, Manage, and Measure Information as an Asset for Competitive Advantage* (Routledge, 2017), written by Gartner's Doug Laney. It is necessary to identify and map out information assets so that confidential information including protected health information (PHI) and personally identifiable information (PII) may be secured directly, so that if hackers are able to get inside the organization's firewall, this information is encrypted and unreadable. The IG steering committee must also explore analytic tools that could help to maximize information value, which may come in the form of reducing medical mistakes and improving patient outcomes, improving patient satisfaction, improving operational efficiency, reducing legal costs, improving compliance capabilities, and other related benefits. In addition, clear policies must be established for the secure access and use of information, and those policies must be communicated regularly and crisply to employees, with constant reinforcement. This includes conveying the value and risk of information, and the consequences of violating IG policies.

2. **Stakeholder consultation**. IG programs are, by nature, cross-functional efforts. Those who work most closely to information are the ones who best know why it is needed and how to manage it, so business units must be consulted in IG policy development. Health information management (HIM) professionals know the details and nuances of managing patient records. They should be deeply involved in electronic health record (EHR) governance efforts, which should be at the core of IG programs in healthcare as saving lives and improving patient outcomes are paramount. Effective EHR governance also leads to reduced costs and improved operational efficiency. So HIM professionals must be an active part of IG programs and their input into the policymaking process is critical. HIM professionals must

also work hand-in-hand with privacy and legal professionals to ensure patient privacy is protected vigilantly. Privacy has become even more important globally with the implementation of Europe's General Data Protection Regulation (GDPR), which applies to any organization conducting business with European citizens, regardless of location. Increased privacy protections for U.S. consumers are also being formed by state legislatures and voter initiatives. In-house legal council should be a key player in IG programs and the legal team must be consulted on a variety of legal, regulatory, privacy, and litigation issues as IG program efforts involve all these areas. Further, IG programs can cut electronic discovery collection and review costs and make the legal hold notification (LHN) process more streamlined and effective. The IT department must play a major role as technology is leveraged in IG program efforts. Healthcare organizations have historically been behind the curve in implementing information technology, compared to other business segments. And healthcare organizations are attacked more frequently by hackers since PHI can be worth more than 10 times what credit card information is worth. This underscores the need for a robust cyber-security program, including security awareness training, to offset information risks. It is clear that cross-functional stakeholder consultation is a necessary component of IG programs.

3. **Information integrity**. The patient–provider relationship is based on trust, and that trust includes ensuring that accurate patient information is created, and also kept secure. IG programs focus heavily on information quality, from the ground up, beginning with data governance. Data governance techniques and tools focus on creating clean, accurate, non-duplicate data in database tables so that downstream reports and analyses are more trusted and accurate. In the U.S., the problem created by the rush to implement EHR systems and show "meaningful use" by the January 1, 2014, deadline (as specified by The American Recovery and Reinvestment Act) was that many systems were implemented without proper planning and as a result, many EHR systems are filled with inaccurate data. This scenario lends itself to increasing the rate of medical mistakes and causing suboptimal outcomes, injury, or even death to patients. Information integrity considers the consistency of methods used to create, retain, preserve, distribute, and track information. Information integrity means there is the assurance that information is accurate, correct, and authentic. From a legal standpoint, enabling information technologies and data stewardship polices must support the effort to meet legal standards of admissibility and preserve the integrity of information to guard against claims that it has been altered, tampered with, or deleted (called "**spoliation**"). Audit trails must be kept and monitored to ensure compliance with IG policies to ensure information integrity.

4. **Information organization and classification**. This means that not only must patient records be organized in a standardized taxonomy with a specified metadata approach, but that all information, including nonclinical business information across the healthcare enterprise must be organized in a standardized way, categorizing all information, and semantically linking it to related information. It also means creating a records retention schedule (RRS) that spells out how long the PHI as well as business information (e.g. e-mail, e-documents, spreadsheets, reports) should be retained and how it is to be disposed of or archived (disposition). Further, it means developing departmental file plans which are logical and help end users conduct more complete and accurate searches for information. More progressive organizations will go further and implement an Information Asset Register (IAR) to track information assets.

5. **Information security and privacy**. This again focuses on the trust proposition between patient and provider. Information security must be in place before information privacy can be assured. This means that every attempt must be made to secure PHI and PII in all three states: at rest, in motion, and in use. It means that the organization should conduct

regular **security awareness training (SAT)**, which can include staged phishing and spear phishing attacks to see if employees handle them properly, and to coach them on mistakes they may make during the test. Ransomware is also a problem. When rogue players launch ransomware attacks, they typically encrypt the storage drives of the healthcare organization and demand a modest payment by bitcoin. *To offset this risk a complete backup of your entire information system must be made daily and kept physically separate from your network, offline.* Additional cyber-security hygiene measures are needed to protect information from damage, theft, or alteration by malicious outsiders and insiders as well as non-malicious (accidental) actions that may compromise information. For instance, an employee may lose a laptop with confidential information, but if proper IG policies are enforced using security-related information technologies, the information can be kept secure. This can be done by access control methods, data or document encryption, deploying information rights management (IRM) software, using remote digital shredding capabilities, and implementing enhanced auditing procedures. Information privacy awareness training should also be conducted, including updates on federal and state legal requirements. Information privacy is closely related to information security and is critical when dealing with PHI and PII and other sensitive information, such as race or religion.

6. **Information accessibility**. Information accessibility must be balanced with information security concerns. Information accessibility includes making the information as simple as possible to locate and access, which involves not only an intuitive user interface but also utilizing enterprise search principles, technologies, and tools. It further includes basic access controls, such as password management, identity and access management (IAM), and delivering information to a variety of hardware devices. Accessibility to information is essential not only in the short term but also over time. Maintaining patient records for perhaps decades requires consideration of long-term digital preservation (LTDP) planning, tools, and methods in accordance with international, technology-neutral standards. Today, LTDP capabilities can be provided through cloud service providers, which keep a number of copies of the information (5–6 typically) on Amazon or Microsoft cloud servers, spread around the world, to reduce the risk of loss. There are privacy implications to this global approach, especially with GDPR legislation, and they must be researched.

7. **Information control**. An enterprise RRS is a key foundational element of IG programs. Non-record information must also be categorized and scheduled. Then a standardized, automated LHN process must be put in place to assign data stewards and lock down information that may be requested in legal proceedings. In addition, key information control technologies must be deployed to control the access, creation, updating, and printing of data, documents, and reports. These technologies include several types of software: EHR, document management, document analytics, report management, and workflow. Additional security software including encryption should be deployed to protect confidential or sensitive information.

8. **Information governance monitoring and auditing**. Early on in the development of an IG program a concerted effort must be made to develop metrics to objectively measure program progress and employee conformance with IG polices. To ensure that guidelines and policies are being followed, especially regarding patient privacy and cyber-security hygiene, information access and use must be monitored. To guard against claims of legal spoliation, the use of e-mail, social media, cloud computing, and report generation should be logged (recorded or archived) in real time and maintained as an audit record. Technology tools such as document analytics can track how many documents users access and print and how long they spend doing so.

9. **Executive sponsorship**. Once again, due to the cross-functional, collaborative nature of IG programs, this is *the most crucial factor in IG program success.* This is especially true in the healthcare arena, where various clinical specialties which may have their own proprietary information systems are represented. No IG effort will survive and be successful if it does not have an accountable, responsible executive sponsor. The sponsor must develop the business case for IG early on, establish a budget, then assemble the steering committee and drive the effort. The executive sponsor must pay periodic attention to the IG program, monitoring progress based on metrics and milestones. The IG program lead, or perhaps even a Chief IG Officer, manages the IG program on a day-to-day basis, bringing in the executive sponsor only when support is needed for a particular issue. The executive sponsor must clear obstacles for the IG program lead and IG steering committee, while actively communicating the goals and business objectives that the IG program addresses, while keeping upper management informed on progress, particularly when accomplishing milestones.

10. **Continuous improvement**. IG programs are not one-time projects but rather ongoing programs, akin to a workplace safety program. (In fact, the information security aspects of an IG program could actually be termed "information safety.") The IG program is a major change management effort, which requires a major training and communications effort. Progress in the IG program must be reviewed periodically and adjusted to account for gaps or shortcomings, as well as changes in the business environment, technology usage, or business strategy.

Using these 10 principles as guidelines will help to communicate with stakeholders and the IG steering committee what IG is, why it is needed, what it involves, and how to fashion an IG program that is successful. It is essential to continually reinforce the importance of these principles during the course of an IG program, and measure how well the organization is doing in these 10 critical areas.

There are also other sets of principles that apply to IG efforts and can help provide a more complete understanding of IG programs, especially early in the IG program development process. These IG principles reflect, reinforce, and expand on the previous sets.

Recordkeeping Principles

Records and information management (RIM) and particularly health information management (HIM) are key facets of an IG program in healthcare, based on surveys of IG professionals and published case studies. In 2009, the records management association ARMA International published a set of eight **Generally Accepted Recordkeeping Principles®**, often referred to as "The Principles"[2] (or sometimes "GAR Principles"), to foster awareness of good recordkeeping practices. These principles have been used as the foundation for a maturity model, which is somewhat mischaracterized as an IG maturity model, since in fact it was clearly developed as a recordkeeping maturity model. As such, the status of organizations' RIM programs can be assessed based on a scale of 1–5, with 1 being the lowest (Substandard) and 5 being the highest (Transformational). When the assessment is complete, an improvement roadmap can be developed to map out the steps needed to improve RIM functions.

In 2014, the American Health Information Management Association (AHIMA), adopted and adapted ARMA's Generally Accepted Recordkeeping Principles® and renamed them, again, somewhat inaccurately, as the **Information Governance Principles for Healthcare®** (IGPHC). Mostly, the words "information governance" have been substituted for "recordkeeping," but the definition of The Principles remains largely the same, and they can be applied to both clinical and nonclinical information recordkeeping across the healthcare enterprise.

The eight IGPHC® are:

1. **Accountability**. A senior executive (or person of comparable authority) oversees the IG program and delegates program responsibility to appropriate individuals.[3]
2. **Transparency**. The processes and activities of an organization's IG program are documented in a manner that is open and verifiable and is available to all personnel and appropriate interested parties. Documentation shall be made readily available to employees and appropriate third parties.
3. **Integrity**. An IG program shall be constructed so the information created, managed, or provided to the organization has a reasonable and suitable guarantee of authenticity and reliability. "*Integrity* of information, which is expected by patients, consumers, stakeholders, and other interested parties such as investors and regulatory agencies, is directly related to the organization's ability to prove that information is *authentic, timely, accurate, and complete*. For the healthcare industry, these dimensions of integrity are essential to ensuring trust in information."[4]
4. **Protection**. An IG program must provide a reasonable level of protection for information against breaches, damage, theft, and internal bad actors, especially for information that is private, confidential, sensitive, secret, classified, or for vital records which are critical to disaster recovery. All information, whether it is electronic or physical (e.g. paper, microfilm) must be appropriately protected from its initial creation through its lifecycle.
5. **Compliance**. The IG program shall be constructed to comply with applicable laws, regulations, standards, and the organization's policies. All organizations must comply with applicable legal and regulatory requirements. "Some healthcare requirements warrant special attention and consideration. For example, laws governing privacy and confidentiality, and fraud and abuse are particularly important to healthcare organizations."[5]
6. **Availability**. An organization shall maintain information in a manner that ensures timely, efficient, and accurate retrieval. Being able to do so impacts stakeholder trust. Securely delivering the right information to the right people at the right time, a key tenet of IG, requires a focus on availability, balancing information access needs with cyber-security and privacy requirements and concerns.
7. **Retention**. An organization shall maintain its information for an appropriate time, taking into account legal, regulatory, fiscal, operational, risk, and historical requirements. Information must be available for retrieval during its active lifecycle, within its retention period. Information lifecycles must be managed for both clinical and nonclinical information, irrespective of its storage medium.
8. **Disposition**. An organization shall provide secure and appropriate disposition for information that is no longer required to be maintained by applicable laws and the organization's policies.[6] Disposition includes not only destruction, but also transfer in ownership or long-term archiving of information. Disposition "applies not only to patient health records and data, but many other types of information such as meeting minutes, credentialing files, agreements, financial records, human resource information, and privileged information such as that related to quality assurance."[7] Bear in mind that business units may request retention of information longer than is required by law or statute, for business reasons such as **knowledge management** (KM), or historical/longitudinal research.

The IGPHC apply to all sizes of healthcare organizations, in both the private and public sectors, and can be used to establish consistent practices across business units.

Information Security Principles

Principle of Least Privilege

The **Principle of Least Privilege** (POLP) is an important cyber-security maxim that means users should only be given access to the bare minimum permissions and information needed to do their job.[8] Under POLP, users are only given access to the files needed to perform their job function. POLP should be used to control who has access to which information, on which devices, and when.

The CIA Triad

The CIA triad (sometimes referred to as the AIC triad to avoid confusion with the U.S. government spy agency) depicts the three "most crucial components" of information security.[9]

Confidentiality (roughly equivalent to IGPHC® #4, Protection) means that access to private and sensitive information is tightly controlled so that only authorized personnel have access to it. **Integrity** (the same as IGPHC® #3) means that information has a reasonable assurance of being accurate, reliable, and trusted, throughout its lifecycle. **Availability** (the same as IGPHC® #6) is the concept that information can be reliably and consistently accessed and retrieved by authorized employees, which requires that software patches and updates are implemented in a timely way, and that hardware is maintained regularly.

Privacy Principles

The **Generally Accepted Privacy Principles** (GAPP) were developed jointly by the Canadian Institute of Chartered Accountants (CICA) and the American Institute of Certified Public Accountants (AICPA) through the AICPA/CICA Privacy Task Force. These principles can be used to guide the privacy aspects of an IG program. The field of information privacy is rapidly changing, and the International Association of Privacy Professionals (IAPP) is quite active globally with conferences, workshops, and training. Nevertheless, the 10 Generally Accepted Privacy Principles have been accepted by the privacy profession. The 10 Generally Accepted Privacy Principles and their criteria are:[10]

1. **Management**
   - The organization defines, documents, communicates and assigns accountability for its privacy policies and procedures.
   - *Criteria*:
     - privacy policies define and document all 10 GAPP
     - review and approval of changes to privacy policies conducted by management
     - risk assessment process in place to establish a risk baseline and regularly identify new or changing risks to personal data
     - infrastructure and systems management takes into consideration impacts on personal privacy
     - privacy awareness training
2. **Notice**
   - The organization provides notice of its privacy policies and procedures. The organization identifies the purposes for which personal information is collected, used and retained.
   - *Criteria*:
     - communication to individuals
     - provision of notice
     - use of clear and conspicuous language
3. **Choice and consent**
   - The organization describes the choices available to the individual. The organization secures implicit or explicit consent regarding the collection, use and disclosure of the personal data.
   - *Criteria*:
     - communicating the consequences of denying/withdrawing consent
     - consent for new purposes/uses of the personal data
     - explicit consent for sensitive data
     - consent for online data transfer
4. **Collection**
   - Personal information is only collected for the purposes identified in the notice (see #2).
   - *Criteria*:
     - document and describe types of information collected and methods of collection
     - collection of information by fair and lawful means, including collection from third parties
     - inform individuals if information is developed or additional information is acquired
5. **Use, retention, and disposal**
   - The personal information is limited to the purposes identified in the notice the individual consented to. The organization retains the personal information only for as long as needed to fulfill the purposes, or as required by law. After this period, the information is disposed of appropriately.

- *Criteria*:
  - systems and procedures in place to ensure personal information is used, retained and disposed appropriately

6. **Access**
   - The organization provides individuals with access to their personal information for review or update.
   - *Criteria*:
     - confirmation of individual's identity before access is given to personal information
     - personal information presented in understandable format
     - access provided in reasonable time frame and at a reasonable cost
     - statement of disagreement; the reason for denial should be explained to individuals in writing

7. **Disclosure to third parties**
   - Personal information is disclosed to third parties only for the identified purposes and with implicit or explicit consent of the individual.
   - *Criteria*:
     - communication with third parties should be made known to the individual
     - information should only be disclosed to third parties that have equivalent agreements to protect personal information
     - individuals should be aware of any new uses/purposes for the information
     - the organization should take remedial action in response to misuse of personal information by a third party

8. **Security for privacy**
   - Personal information is protected against both physical and logical unauthorized access.
   - *Criteria*:
     - privacy policies must address the security of personal information
     - information security programs must include administrative, technical and physical safeguards
     - logical access controls in place
     - restrictions on physical access
     - environmental safeguards
     - personal information protected when being transmitted (e.g. mail, Internet, public or other non-secure networks)
     - security safeguards should be tested for effectiveness at least once annually

9. **Quality**
   - The organization maintains accurate, complete and relevant personal information that is necessary for the purposes identified.
   - *Criteria*:
     - personal information should be relevant for the purposes it is being used

10. **Monitoring and enforcement**
    - The organization monitors compliance with its privacy policies and procedures. It also has procedures in place to address privacy-related complaints and disputes.

- *Criteria*:
  - individuals should be informed on how to contact the organization with inquiries, complaints and disputes
  - formal process in place for inquires, complaints or disputes
  - each complaint is addressed and the resolution is documented for the individual
  - compliance with privacy policies, procedures, commitments and legislation is reviewed, documented and reported to management

These 10 principles can be applied by healthcare organizations to establish and maintain the privacy aspects of their IG programs.

Utilizing the various sets of complementary IG principles to help educate stakeholders and guide the IG program will help to keep the scope of the program focused by providing some guidelines to keep it on track that help ensure the success of the program.

Chapter Summary: Key Points

- **The Sedona Conference Commentary on Information Governance provides 11 principles to consider when implementing IG programs.**
- Cross-functional collaboration is needed for IG policies to hit the mark and be effective.
- Lines of authority, accountability, and responsibility must be clear for the IG program to succeed.
- Adhering to good IG practices includes data governance techniques and technologies to ensure quality data.
- Information form and formats should be standardized and classified according to a corporate taxonomy.
- Sensitive information must be secured its three states: at rest, in motion, and in use.
- Information accessibility includes making it as simple as possible to locate and access info.
- Deploy software to control the access to, creation, updating, and printing of information.
- Information access and use must be monitored and audited, especially regarding confidential and sensitive information.
- No IG effort will survive and be successful if it does not have an accountable, responsible executive sponsor.
- IG programs are not one-time projects but rather ongoing programs.
- AHIMA's Information Governance Principles for Healthcare® (IGPH) can be used to guide HIM programs and as a general reference for HIM and RIM aspects of IG programs.
- The Principle of Least Privilege (POLP) is an important cyber-security maxim that means users should only be given access to the bare minimum permissions and information needed to do their job.
- The CIA information security triad includes Confidentiality, Integrity, and Availability, three principles which can be mapped back to the IGPH® from AHIMA.
- Patient privacy is a major issue in healthcare and a key aspect of IG programs. Privacy considerations should be injected into daily business processes. The 10 Generally Accepted Privacy Principles provide guidance for privacy programs.

Notes

1. "The Sedona Conference Commentary on Information Governance," The Sedona Conference, October 2014, https://thesedonaconference.org/publication/The%20Sedona%20Conference%C2%AE%20Commentary%20on%20Information%20Governance.
2. "Generally Accepted Recordkeeping Principles," ARMA International, 2009, www.arma.org/garp/copyright.cfm.
3. "Information Governance Principles for Healthcare (IGPHC)," AHIMA, 2014, http://www.ahima.org/~/media/AHIMA/Files/HIM-Trends/IG_Principles.ashx.
4. Ibid.
5. Ibid.
6. "Information Governance Maturity Model," ARMA International, 2009, www.arma.org/garp/Garp%20maturity%20Model%20Grid%20(11x23).pdf.
7. "Information Governance Principles for Healthcare (IGHC)," AHIMA, 2014, http://www.ahima.org/~/media/AHIMA/Files/HIM-Trends/IG_Principles.ashx.
8. Margaret Rouse, "Principle of Least Privilege," TechTarget.com, http://searchsecurity.techtarget.com/definition/principle-of-least-privilege-POLP.
9. Margaret Rouse, "Confidentiality, Integrity, and Availability (CIA Triad)," TechTarget.com, http://whatis.techtarget.com/definition/Confidentiality-integrity-and-availability-CIA.
10. "Generally Accepted Privacy Principles (GAPP," CIPPGuide.org, https://www.cippguide.org/2010/07/01/generally-accepted-privacy-principles-gapp/.

Chapter 4

Who Should Be Part of an Information Governance Team?

IG programs require cross-functional collaboration; however, IG teams or steering committees from each individual healthcare organization will have a slightly different makeup depending on program focus and objectives, organizational IG maturity, staffing, budget resources, competitive posture, and other factors.

A formal IG **Program Charter** must be drafted and signed off on by the executive sponsor. The program charter lays out the purpose and scope of the program, goals and objectives, reporting structure of the IG steering committee, SMEs and sub-committees, frequency of meeting, and other key guidelines.

Selection of the executive sponsor is a critical starting point. The executive sponsor must make the business case for the IG program and make IG steering committee selections along with the IG Lead. It is advisable that a deputy or associate executive sponsor also be named to build in durability and continuity to the IG program, in the event that the executive sponsor leaves or is terminated. This is also true of the IG Lead.

IG Is an Umbrella Program

IG can be thought of as an overall umbrella program that manages or "governs" information access, risk, quality, protection, privacy, and the information lifecycle across the enterprise. IG is a broad policy framework for enforcing information compliance and accountability, with progress measured by agreed-upon metrics. These metrics must be developed with the input of stakeholders so that they are not only relevant and meaningful, but also accepted by the end users and IG team members.

Having better quality and more trusted information helps improve decision-making and compliance capabilities while reducing information risk. Formally embedding an IG program ensures that resources, including budget and management time, are spent to maximize information value while minimizing information risks and costs.

Leveraging Models and Frameworks

There are several IG models and frameworks that can help to inform the selection and development of an IG steering committee.

The IG Reference Model

The core IG steering committee group must include Legal, IT, HIM and RIM, Cyber-security, and Privacy, at a minimum, provided the organization has these basic functions represented in the organizational structure. (And if these functions are not represented in an organization of today, they should be).

There is precedent for this foundational structure, when looking at the Information Governance Reference Model (IGRM). The IGRM is a simple graphic tool developed by EDRM.net, ARMA International, and the Compliance, Governance, & Oversight Council (CGOC) in consultation with thousands of end users. The IGRM graphically displays the key impact areas of IG programs, shows unified governance and process transparency, and depicts the relationship between information assets, duty, and value, which can help to educate IG program stakeholders early on and to spur discussion of IG's cross-functional nature.[1]

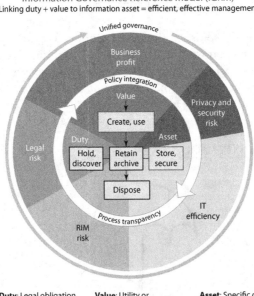

Information Governance Reference Model (IGRM)
Linking duty + value to information asset = efficient, effective management

| **Duty**: Legal obligation for specific information | **Value**: Utility or business purpose of specific information | **Asset**: Specific container of information |

Take note that there is one more group depicted, which is "Business" or business units. The key business unit(s) included in the IG program may reflect a focus on data governance, EHR governance, patient privacy, or reducing legal costs, and will vary based on a particular healthcare organization's structure, business objectives, and business scenario. Business units provide critical input in IG policy development efforts.

HIM and the governance of EHR information are fundamental to reducing medical mistakes, improving patient outcomes, improving patient satisfaction and retention, reducing litigation and associated costs, and improving overall population health. There may be other business units that are high priority, such as the Business Office function, where improvements in operational efficiency can yield significant economic benefits. Beyond that, business units with the highest litigation costs or most difficulty with finding information for everyday tasks, litigation requests, or compliance audits are good places to look for high priority pilot projects under the umbrella of the overall lG program.

Some additional key departments that should be represented on the next tier of the IG steering committee, (depending on the organizational structure and business scenario), may be:

- **Finance/CFO**. Often overlooked is the idea that poor IG can lead to major data breaches and dramatic losses in patient/customer confidence, revenues, and market value of the organization. The case can be made that the CFO shares a fiduciary responsibility to ensure that proper IG controls are in place to help safeguard the organization's information assets. Also, the CFO will know the status of budgets and can possibly make adjustments or transfers to invest in needed IG program steps. And once IG controls are in place, Infonomics principles may be applied to gain new value or even monetize information.
- **Chief Data Officer (CDO)/Data governance**. As quality clinical data is critical for delivering value and improving patient outcomes and overall population health, this is a key role. All other downstream reports and analytics depend on having clean, accurate, non-duplicate data, so it is critical to have a data governance effort that focuses on capturing accurate data at the source. This can be challenging in healthcare, with the variety of proprietary clinical and laboratory devices that do not always adhere to industry standard data formats.
- **Risk management**. Managing information risk is core to IG efforts. You can see "Risk" noted as a focus in the IGRM graphic under "Legal," "Privacy & Security," and "RIM." If the organization has a formal risk management department, their involvement in the IG program will be valuable. Some organizations may wish to use the ISO 31000 Risk Management standard to guide efforts.
- **Compliance**. HIPAA compliance is critical and HIPAA audits can result in major fines. Compliance efforts focus both externally, regarding regulations and statutory requirements, and internally, to ensure employees follow company policies and procedures, as well as externally imposed requirements.
- **Human resources**. Since IG programs are change management (CM) efforts, HR is central to the communications and training strategy to help embed IG considerations like privacy and security into routine business processes. Emphasizing compliance with IG policies and procedures in employee performance reviews will involve working with HR to develop meaningful metrics. Training should be conducted regularly and consistently, using multiple modalities.
- **Change management**. If the organization has a formal CM function, this group can play a key role, as *all IG programs are fundamentally CM efforts*. Often an external consultant can assist in developing the CM plan to complement IG efforts.

■ **Analytics**. Applying advanced analytics to clean, accurate data can yield a variety of benefits in healthcare, namely the improvement of clinical outcomes and financial performance. Additional advances can be made in improving patient satisfaction and perhaps even some new insights and innovations in patient care. Further, there may be new ways to improve operational efficiency, and beyond that, monetize and leverage aggregated or anonymized data with suppliers or business partners. "Harnessing the value of information is one of the foundational purposes of IG, but an IG program also must balance the goals of analytics against information risks and retention requirements."[2]

■ **Audit**. The Audit department can play a key role in measuring IG program progress based on meaningful, pre-established metrics which have been developed and approved by the IG team. Metrics provide management feedback for continual improvement and program fine-tuning. Audit findings can provide crucial input for decision-making within an IG program.

Introducing the Information Governance Adoption Model™ for Healthcare

In February, 2016, AHIMA launched healthcare's first **Information Governance Adoption Model™** (IGAM) via **IGHealthRate™**, an assessment tool.[3] The IGAM is an extension and expansion of the IG Reference Model, although it does not go so far as to diagram inter-relationships and reflect the roles of risk (specifically, information risk) and change management, which are key components of IG programs.

The IG Adoption Model™ can help spur discussion in the beginning stages of IG program planning, and *can also assist in highlighting key areas for representation in the IG Program Steering Committee.*

According to AHIMA, the 10 IG organizational competencies depicted in the model can be assessed based on key markers on a scale of IGAM Level 1™ (lowest, least mature) to IGAM Level 5™ (highest), to determine maturity levels and to conduct a gap analysis to determine the tasks needed to move the organization up the maturity scale to the desired level of improvement.

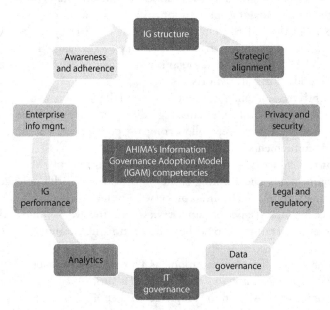

Analyzing the IGAM™ for IG Team Staffing

In the IGAM™ we can see that, as with the IG Reference Model, Privacy and Security are represented, as is Legal & Regulatory. Also, Data Governance and Analytics are represented, furthering the argument to include representation of these functions on the IG steering committee. IT governance, that is, leveraging frameworks (e.g. CoBIT5) in the IT department to make it more efficient and accountable, while getting results that contribute to organizational business objectives, is also represented. The employee in charge of IT governance, likely the CIO, should be considered a major stakeholder. The CIO is also accountable for enterprise information management (EIM), a major aspect of IG.

IG structure and strategic alignment are mostly responsibilities of the executive sponsor and IG Lead, with input from the entire committee. IG performance could be measured quantitatively by the CFO or an internal audit professional, and monitored by the Executive Sponsor.

IG awareness is largely the job of the Executive Sponsor and IG Lead, with assistance from HR or the training department. IG Adherence and IG Performance should be monitored by the Executive Sponsor using established metrics, perhaps audited by the CFO or an internal auditor.

In Summary

It is abundantly clear that implementing IG programs *requires a cross-functional approach* to facilitate sharing and leveraging information. IG has a wide reach and effective IG brings together stakeholders from across the organization and builds on their synergies to better govern and optimize information.

Information governance programs are heavily focused on information quality, security, and privacy. As a cross-functional discipline, it is challenging to muster and manage scarce resources to address enterprise issues that do not belong clearly to established functional groups like IT or Legal. Managing and prioritizing these information asset challenges requires the same type of planning and control used historically for deploying and managing capital assets. Managing and leveraging information assets means that new opportunities and value may be found that can provide a sustainable competitive advantage to the organization.[4]

Major Executive Sponsor Role

Throughout this book, one key fact is emphasized repeatedly: Securing a sponsor at the executive management level is critical—it is the *most important factor for IG success*. In fact, it is so important it may be advisable to name a separate deputy executive sponsor, or to have the IG steering committee chair also serve as a deputy or co-executive sponsor.

Strong executive sponsorship is a key IG Best Practice. Program failure is a great risk without an active and engaged executive sponsor. Such a program likely will fade or fizzle out or be relegated to the back burner. Without strong high-level leadership, when things go awry, finger pointing and political games may take over, impeding progress and cooperation.

According to studies, the two most common IG executive sponsors are General Counsel and the CIO. Sometimes IG programs are led by an organization's General Counsel, and they may be well-versed in privacy law, but they may not have the technology competencies to understand exactly how to apply complex new IG-enabling technologies, and they may have a basic understanding of retention schedules but are not well-versed in HIM Best Practices. Sometimes IG programs are led by the CIO, who may be well-versed in security and aware of privacy issues, but often CIOs and HIM managers don't speak the same language: a "record" means something totally different to a CIO than to a HIM manager; also, legal research is not the CIO's job and the general counsel will always have to make those decisions anyway.

Executives must be on board and a primary executive sponsor driving the IG effort is needed in order to garner the necessary resources to develop and execute the strategic IG plan. That executive must be held accountable for the development and execution of the plan.

Resources are needed—time, human capital, budget money, new technologies. The first is a critical element: It is not possible to require managers to take time out of their other duties to participate in a project if there is no executive edict and consistent follow-up, support, and communication. In fact, *IG program progress should be measured in performance reviews of key players on the IG steering committee and for stakeholder groups.*

The executive sponsor serves at least six key purposes in an IG program:

1. **Budget.** The executive sponsor ensures an adequate financial commitment is made to see that project milestones are met and lobbies for additional expenditures when change orders are made or cost overruns occur.
2. **Planning and control.** The executive sponsor sets direction and tracks accomplishment of specific, measurable business objectives.
3. **Decision-making.** The executive sponsor makes or approves crucial decisions and resolves issues that are escalated for resolution.
4. **Expectation management.** The executive sponsor must manage expectation, since success is quite often a stakeholder perception.
5. **Anticipation.** Every project that is competing for resources can run into unforeseen blockages and objections. Executive sponsors run interference and provide political might for the IG Lead or **program manager** (PM) to lead the project to completion, through a series of milestones.
6. **Approvals.** The executive sponsor signs off when milestones and objectives have been met and signs contracts for the acquisition of new information technologies and services.

The higher level the executive sponsor is in the organization, the better. The CEO wields the most authority, and some IG programs are sponsored by the CEO, particularly where there has been a major breach, costly litigation, or major regulatory fines. With CEO sponsorship come many of the key elements needed to complete any successful project, including allocated management time, management priority, and budget money.

Critical and Sometimes Fickle Executive Sponsor Role

There may be a clear executive sponsor at some point early on but when that person realizes they will be held accountable for the performance of groups outside their direct control (and competitors at their corporate level can then sabotage progress), they might look for cover and find a way to postpone, de-prioritize, or kill the IG program. *Focusing efforts on clearly established business objectives will largely reduce this inherent problem of conflicting agendas.* (Having a deputy executive sponsor will also shore up the executive sponsor role).

Sometimes all an unenthusiastic executive sponsor has to do is wait for the natural inertia of the over-sized and lethargic IG steering committee to weigh things down, and soon other projects and programs that are more routine and cost-justifiable in the short term take resources from the

IG effort. It then may fade into the background until there is a new litigation disaster, major compliance failure, massive security breach, or other such negative IG drivers.

According to surveys and research, the implementation of an IG program is more and more often being driven by the Legal department, General Counsel or Assistant General Counsel, or the chief information officer (CIO). Other IG programs may be led by the chief risk officer, chief information security officer (CISO), or, ideally, as the Sedona Conference has recommended, a Chief IG Officer (CIGO).

The CIGO must have the mandate and authority to drive the program forward and should have overlapping skillsets that include expertise in e-discovery, cyber-security, information privacy, data governance, health information management (HIM) and general records management, IT, and business operations.

The Emerging Role of the CIGO

A key challenge is that because of the interdisciplinary requirements for implementing IG, no one seems to want to *own* IG. It touches on parts of the strengths of a CIO or General Counsel or HIM Manager or Information Security Manager or Chief Compliance Officer, but it also requires that they go out of their comfort zone into new areas.

So where should IG reside? Who should be in charge of an IG program?

There is a need for a new job title to pull all these disciplines together into a cohesive IG program: CIGO. This has been promoted by the Sedona Conference® and other organizations.

The CIGO should be a highly competent manager who has broad operations experience and competencies: near-expert not only in IT, but also legal and compliance issues, data governance tools and methods, HIM issues, privacy issues, information security tools and techniques, and business issues. They must also have outstanding communications and management skills. That is a challenging job description.

A CIGO can act in a coordinating function, but lacking authority, their efforts will likely be met with resistance. Because of its requirements, the organization can leverage the authority of the executive sponsor, or even consider granting the CIGO authority over the CIO, chief information security officer (CISO), chief privacy officer (CPO), and even CFO. The CIGO could be very nearly a chief operations officer (COO), and that is an option for whom the CIGO reports to, if not the EVP of Risk—or even the Administrator or CEO. It is a crucial job that mostly is not being filled. However, there is a great need for it, and it due to its focus, a well-prepared CIGO could lead the IG effort and produce consistent, tangible results.

Assigning Team Roles and Responsibilities

The executive sponsor must designate an IG Lead or program manager—perhaps even a Chief IG Officer—and depending on the focus of the IG effort, that person could come from one of several areas including legal, infosec, risk management, HIM/records management, or IT.

When assigning the roles and responsibilities of the remainder of the IG team, the easy decision is to have IG team representatives take responsibility for the functional areas of their expertise. Nevertheless, there will be overlap, and it is best to have some pairs or small workgroups teamed up to gain the broadest amount of input and optimum results.

This will also facilitate cross-training. For instance, inside legal counsel may be responsible for rendering the final legal opinions, but not being an expert in HIM or document management or risk management means they could benefit from input of others in specialized functional areas, which will inform them and help narrow and focus their legal research. So when performing the basic research as to which regulations and laws apply to the organization regarding security, retention, and preservation of patient records and PII, the initial research could be conducted by the HIM or records management head, in consultation with the corporate archivist and CIO, with the results of their findings and recommendations drafted and sent to the legal counsel. The draft report may offer up several alternative approaches that need legal input and decisions. Then the legal department can conduct their own, focused research, and make final recommendations with consideration given to the organization's legal strategy, business objectives, financial position, and applicable laws and regulations.

The result of the research, consultation, and collaboration of the IG team should be a final draft of the IG strategic plan (see Chapter 9 for more detail). It will still need more input and development to align the plan with business objectives, an analysis of internal and external drivers, applicable Best Practices, competitive analysis, applicable information technology trends, an analysis and inclusion of the organization's culture, and other factors.

Caveat: The Importance of a Tiered IG Steering Committee for Expediency

When reviewing research and anecdotal observations on IG programs it is clear that often IG efforts are slow to start, can get delayed or put on hold, and then re-start, and that sometimes the IG effort is abandoned, put on a shelf. Then later, executives realize that the "IG problem" (e.g. deaths and injury from medical mistakes, non-compliance fines, risks of colossal information breaches, soaring litigation costs, failure to capitalize on emerging opportunities by leveraging analytics) is not going away—so the IG program re-starts again.

One of the root causes of sluggish IG efforts is the basic failure to structure the IG steering committee properly, and to consider the realities of group dynamics, corporate politics, scheduling, and program management.

Since IG efforts are by nature cross-functional and require the involvement of key stakeholder groups, IG steering committees can become large and unwieldy. Also, the politics can become crippling, causing progress to slow and threatening the continuation of the IG program.

In practice, there have been IG steering committees of 15, 18, even 20 or more individuals representing the various functional groups in a large organization. Managing the needs and inputs of this broad swath of stakeholders is inherently challenging.

Due to the expanse of an IG program, the IG program team or steering committee should be set up with a tiered structure. The core departments driving the IG program, or "top tier" should be:[5]

- **Legal**. Because legal considerations are paramount, the legal department must be deeply involved and perhaps lead the IG program. Legal is best represented at a high level by the General Counsel, Assistant GC, or a senior legal officer. Legal costs and liabilities can soar with poor IG, further underscoring the importance of efficient legal functions. Further, Legal must implement "litigation response protocols" and drive e-discovery efforts—which inherently involve IT and records management policies, two other core stakeholders in IG programs. The legal department also must provide guidance on privacy breach response protocols and render opinions on privacy matters to ensure compliance.
- **Information technology**. IT is key to IG efforts, as IG requires IT for data and IT governance, and for tracking sensitive information, applying automated controls, auditing,

implementing business process redesign, and more. Organizations must leverage IT to improve efficiencies and monitor the effectiveness of the IG program. Also, IT must work with Legal, HIM, and RIM to preserve the organization's electronically stored information (ESI) in legal matters.

■ **Health Information Management (HIM) and Records and Information Management (RIM).** The HIM department is responsible for managing patient health records in accordance with privacy laws and retention regulations. Safeguarding these records is mission-critical and a key factor in maintaining patient trust. RIM is responsible for maintaining corporate business records to ensure compliance with applicable statutory and regulatory requirements. HIM and RIM must also work with Legal to execute e-discovery functions.

■ **Information Security.** "InfoSec" or "cyber-security" is responsible for keeping the organization's databases and confidential information secure, and providing policy input, techniques, and IT to prevent the loss of intellectual property (IP). InfoSec has played an increasingly greater role in IG programs due to colossal data breaches, privacy concerns, and reputational risk;

■ **Privacy.** The Privacy group must conduct research and provide policy guidance for the handling of protected health information (PHI), personally identifiable information (PII), credit card information (PCI), and other sensitive patient and employee information. The goal is to have privacy considerations "baked in" to everyday business processes, so that, "privacy by design" may be achieved.[6] This is a key aim of IG programs.

The *tiered strategy* can be employed to make these IG planning teams more effective, agile, and accountable: A tiered IG steering committee with staggered meeting requirements will bring in only those needed to a meeting, while not wasting everyone else's time.

Otherwise, the IG program initiative will follow the same predictable and sluggish cycle it did before, only with a slightly different set of players.

Below are some guidelines for structuring an IG steering committee for better results:

1. **Recruit a strong executive sponsor (and perhaps a deputy executive sponsor).** A clear leader who has authority can help focus IG efforts and deliver results in the form of early wins to keep feeding and growing the IG program. The executive sponsor should be apprised of progress and should sign off on milestones and major policy decisions as they are presented to them by a small subset of leaders from the IG steering committee. Due to the importance of the executive sponsor, and the fact that turnover does occur and can hinder program progress, it is advisable to consider naming a "deputy" executive sponsor as a backup support.

2. **Form a high-level "decision committee."** This can be a group of three, four, or at the most, five leaders from the functional areas most involved in IG efforts. They are the ones who are to be held accountable for delivering results and keeping the IG program on track. They should meet regularly, probably weekly, to drive the IG program forward. Their focus should be on *focus,* that is, directing the efforts of the IG steering committee and delegating specific tasks to ensure tangible results are delivered from small early wins and the IG program expands in a logical way that focuses on meeting business objectives.

3. **Form subject matter expert (SME) teams** using cross-functional team members. In a sort of matrix organizational structure, create teams to center effort on key areas of IG impact, and to cross-train each other. For instance, the e-discovery readiness team should include members from Legal staff, but also (depending on the business scenario) HIM, Records Management, IT, and perhaps the business unit that is most involved or embroiled in litigation. The Data Governance (DG) SME team must include the DG lead, but also members

from Privacy, Security, IT, and key business units. Recommendations from the SME teams should be made to the decision committee for final deliberation, and then presented to the executive sponsor for sign-off and approval (or rejection to re-work the approach).

4. **Keep all members of the IG steering committee updated**. Committee members should be regularly updated on program status, progress, and decisions. Do not waste committee members' time with a meeting when an e-mail or update to the intranet or collaborative site will do.

5. **Convene the entire IG steering group only when necessary**—perhaps every two weeks in the initial phases of the IG program, and then at least monthly following the IG program launch. The meeting of the entire group should be scheduled so that it does not conflict with IG steering committee members' schedules to the extent possible.

Additional tips: For those who cannot attend a formal IG program meeting, provide a video conference or at least a conference call link, and for those who cannot attend even remotely, a recording of the meeting. Do not allow excuses for non-participation. Also, ensure that tasks and progress of the IG program effort are tied directly to stated business objectives.

Stay focused and do not waste IG steering committee members' time. Lay out a reporting and meeting schedule that makes sense and structure the IG team into more agile, accountable units which can meet on their own and not waste others' time.

Chapter Summary: Key Points

- **Implementing IG programs requires a cross-functional approach.**
- The IG Reference Model provides a starting point for IG steering committee staffing.
- The IG Adoption Model™ from AHIMA can assist in IG steering committee staffing decisions, and also in planning and IG maturity assessments.
- The top tier of an IG steering committee should include: Legal, IT, HIM/RIM, Information Security, and Privacy.
- A tiered IG steering committee keeps it more nimble and able to make decisions.
- Due to the interdisciplinary requirements for implementing IG, no one wants to *own* IG.
- IG programs require a strong executive sponsor.
- Chief IG Officer (CIGO) is a new title for a person heading up IG programs.
- The CIGO must be proficient in legal issues, cyber-security, HIM, privacy, and more.

Notes

1. "Information Governance Reference Model," EDRM.net, https://www.edrm.net/frameworks-and-standards/information-governance-reference-model.
2. Jason R. Baron and Amy R. Marcos, "Information Governance: Establishing a Program and Executing Initial Projects," *Practical Law*, October/November 2015, 24–33 (pp. 27–28).
3. "Information Governance Offers a Strategic Approach for Healthcare (Updated)," Practice Brief, *Journal of AHIMA* 86, no. 11 (November 2015): 56–59.
4. Ibid.
5. Jason R. Baron and Amy R. Marcos, "Information Governance: Establishing a Program and Executing Initial Projects," *Practical Law*, October/November 2015, 24–33 (p. 26).
6. Ann Cavoukian, "The 7 Foundational Principles," PrivacyByDesign.ca, January 2011, https://www.ipc.on.ca/wp-content/uploads/Resources/7foundationalprinciples.pdf.

Chapter 5

Building an IG Framework

Information Governance is complex and has many "moving parts" due to its cross-functional, collaborative nature. To direct and manage an IG program properly, an **Information Governance Framework** (IGF) must be formally established to provide the guardrails to guide decisions.

An IGF includes, at a minimum:

It is essential that the IGF is customized for each individual healthcare organization and its business needs. The focus of an IG program may vary, and so the structure of the IGF will also vary to reflect that focus.

Building an IG Framework

Once the executive sponsor is in place, (and perhaps a deputy executive sponsor, for good measure), you must build an IGF, which is the foundation of the IG program. Without it, the result will be a weak and unstable, aimless program that will likely fail, as many have.

Each IG framework will look a little different but there are commonalities that appear in successful ones. An IGF needs to be modified according to the business and economic environment, competitive scenario, budget, and internal human resources and skillsets.

Below are the key components of an IG Framework that serve as the construct, the foundation for any successful IG program:

■ **Business objectives** – IG planning must begin with a focus on business objectives. Organizational goals and objectives are the key reason for implementing an IG program. They provide the business rationale for investing resources. *The objectives for the IG program must align with and support the organization's overall strategic plan and IT strategy.* Objectives must then be broken down into measureable, relevant metrics to track progress. Key objectives for healthcare concerns may be:

  – Lower deaths due to medical mistakes by 10% over the previous five year average, within two years;
  – Reduce e-discovery litigation costs by 20% per GB for document review, within one year;
  – Reduce lost, stolen, or compromised mobile devices by 50% over the previous year.
  – Beyond stated, measureable objectives, there may be longer-term goals the organization strives for that the IG program can help support, such as:
    • Deliver premium patient care with unwavering attention to personal privacy;
    • Optimize HIPAA compliance capabilities;
    • Harvest anonymized patient data and leverage Big Data tools for research and analysis, to improve patient care.

■ **Executive sponsor** – This is the manager with the budget authority and the motivation to build the IG program. The executive sponsor is involved with developing the blueprint and overall building plan but leaves the specifics to those with expertise in key areas. She or he stays in the loop, and, at times, may have to intervene. However, at other times, the executive sponsor is the one offering coffee and donuts in the morning or springing for a pizza party on a Friday afternoon after a long week of work where good progress was made. A good executive sponsor uses both carrots and sticks. More information on executive sponsorship is presented later in this chapter, since it is such a critical piece of IG program success.

■ **IG Lead** – The IG Lead must be a talented individual with a diverse skillset. They may come from one of the core areas of IG, such as IT, Information Security, Legal, HIM, or Information Privacy, but they also must be conversant in the other complementary disciplines. In addition, they must have excellent interpersonal skills, as this person must be a change agent, actively promoting and selling the IG program, helping to embed it into the corporate culture. The IG Lead is accountable for executing the IG strategic plan on a day-to-day basis. They must orchestrate the completion of milestones within the budget, resource, and time constraints approved by the executive sponsor. When the IG Lead runs into roadblocks, they should bring in the executive sponsor for support.

■ **Cross-functional IG team** – Just as architects, bricklayers, plumbers, electricians, and carpenters are needed to build a house, an IG program will need a blend of professionals. They should be leaders in key functional areas, including IT, Legal, HIM, Privacy, and Information Security—but also business unit heads/information owners, and potentially other key areas such as Change Management, Risk Management, Communications, Training, and other specialties as appropriate. IG team representation will vary, as organizations have differing corporate structures and cultures, and so business objectives, resources, appetite for risk, and other variables are different, even for similar healthcare entities operating in the same region.

■ **Standards and Best Practices** – A review of relevant standards and Best Practices should be done to determine which ones to select to help guide the IG program.

■ **Survey and evaluation of external factors** – Once the IG team is in place and the IG plan is harmonized and aligned with the organization's strategic plan and IT strategy, good progress will have been made. In evaluating external factors, take into consideration the economic and

competitive business environment, technology trends and developments, regulatory and legislative issues, and even the political environment, which could affect pending regulatory demands.
■ **IG reference models or frameworks** – Survey and select key IG models and frameworks to help guide decisions.
■ **Program metrics, monitoring, auditing, and enforcement** – An IG program must have established metrics and controls to determine the level of employee compliance, its impact on key operational areas, and progress made toward key business objectives. Testing and auditing provide an opportunity to give feedback to employees on how well they are doing and to recommend changes they may make. In addition, having objective feedback on key metrics also will allow the executive sponsor to see where progress has been made, where improvements need to focus, and where resources are needed.
■ **Program communications and training** – IG programs must include a communications and training component as a standard function. The stakeholder audience must be made aware of new policies and practices that are to be followed, and how this new approach contributes toward accomplishing business objectives. This assists in the change management effort. But critically, *stakeholders must receive training on the new approach,* and constant and consistent reinforcement of new IG precepts.

By including the above elements in the IG framework, the organization will have established a solid foundation to build the IG program, and it will have greatly increased its odds of success.

IG Leaders in Healthcare

Leading healthcare organizations that have implemented IG programs share some common characteristics:[1]

1. **Value information as an asset** – Understand the value and risks of information and strive to link information value to organizational objectives;
2. **Collaborative culture** – Recognize that interdisciplinary cooperation is key, and that clinical and business process owners must have strong support from IT, Legal, HIM/RIM, Privacy/Security;
3. **Strong executive sponsorship** – Executives understand the linkage between quality information and quality patient care, and understand that minimizing information risks protects patient trust, brand equity, and shareholder value;
4. **Operational efficiency focus** – Organizational competence in policymaking, business process design, and process improvement;
5. **Continuous improvement ethos** – A cultural commitment to be a learning organization where continual improvement is valued and reinforced.

Executive Sponsor Role versus IG Program Manager

The role of an executive sponsor is high level, requiring periodic and regular attention to the status of the program, particularly with budget issues, staff resources, and milestone progress.

The role of a project or program manager is more detailed and day-to-day, tracking specific tasks that must be executed to make progress toward milestones. Both roles are essential. The savvy PM brings in the executive sponsor to push things along when more authority is needed but reserves such program political capital for those issues that absolutely cannot be resolved without executive intervention. It is best for the PM to keep the executive sponsor fully informed but to ask for assistance only when absolutely needed.

The PM must manage the relationship with the executive sponsor, perhaps with some gentle reminders, coaxing, or prodding, to ensure that the role and major tasks of executive sponsorship are being fulfilled. The successful PM monitors progress and collects data to support their case to the executive sponsor. If the executive sponsor is losing interest or becomes less responsive, it is up to the PM to have a heart-to-heart talk with them to get the program back on track or consider abandoning it.

An eager and effective executive sponsor makes all the difference to a program—if the role is properly managed by the PM. It is a tricky relationship, since the PM is always below the executive sponsor in the organization's hierarchy, yet the PM must coax the superior into tackling certain high-level tasks. Sometimes a third-party consultant who is an expert in the specific project can support requests made of the executive sponsor and provide a solid business rationale.

While the executive sponsor role is high level, the PM's role and tasks are more detailed and involve day-to-day management.

Evolving Role of the Executive Sponsor

The role of the executive sponsor necessarily evolves and changes over the life of the initial IG program launch, during the implementation phases, and on through the continued IG program.

To get the program off the ground, the executive sponsor must first *own the business case*. They must make a solid business case and obtain adequate budgetary funding and resources.

Some cost savings as a result of direct actions within the IG program can add to the cost/benefit analysis. Yet an IG effort requires more than budget money; it takes *time*—not just time to develop new policies, redesign processes, and implement new technologies, but the time of the designated PM, program leaders, and needed program team members.

In order to get this time set aside, the IG program must be a top priority of the organization. It must be recognized, formalized, and *aligned with organizational business objectives*. The up-front work of making the business case and aligning the IG program with business objectives is the responsibility of the executive sponsor.

Communications and Training Plan Is Key

Once the business case is made and the IG steering committee is formed, team members must clearly understand why the new program is important and how it will help the organization meet its business objectives. This message must be regularly communicated and reinforced by the executive sponsor; he or she must not only paint the vision of the future state of the organization but articulate the steps in the path to get there.

When the formal program effort commences, *the executive sponsor must remain visible and accessible*. They cannot disappear into everyday duties and expect the program team to carry the effort through. The executive sponsor must be there to help the team confront and overcome business obstacles as they arise and must praise the successes along the way. This requires active involvement and a willingness to spend the time to keep the program on track and focused.

The executive sponsor must be the lighthouse that shows the way even through cloudy skies and rough waters. This person is the captain who must steer the ship, even if the first mate (PM) is seasick and the deckhands (IG program team) are drenched and tired.

The multi-modal IG program communications strategy should be reinforced through consistent and regular training on IG program aspects.

After the program is implemented, the executive sponsor is responsible for maintaining its effectiveness and relevance. This is done through periodic compliance audits based on pre-established metrics, utilizing testing and sampling, and holding scheduled meetings with the ongoing PM.

IG Requires Change Management

It is important to bear in mind that an IG effort is truly a *change management* effort, in that it aims to change the work processes, guidelines, and information access rules within which clinicians and business process owners operate. It may even change the user interface to systems and the way they work through everyday business processes.

The overall cultural change—one that values information as an asset and seeks to protect and leverage it—must occur at the very core of the organization's culture.

It must be embedded permanently, and for it to be, the message must be constantly and consistently reinforced. Achieving this kind of change requires commitment from the very highest levels of the organization and a planned change management effort.

Which Technologies Help to Enable IG Programs and Enforce Controls?

This section presents a brief overview of the key IG-enabling information technologies that help implement and monitor new information-related processes. These are some of the technologies that the IG Lead and steering committee should be tracking.

Beginning with a compact definition of IG, the technologies are listed in its three key areas.

IG, in short, is defined as "security, control, and optimization of information." This is a concise definition yet it covers a wide expanse. Listed below are some categories of products that may be leveraged in IG programs. This is not an exhaustive list but rather a demonstrative one.

First, "Security" of information:

1. **Electronic document security** – Technologies in this group include information rights management (IRM), and its little brother, file encryption. IRM technology acts like a "security wrapper" that, upon creation, secures confidential e-documents by controlling the "rights" to view, print, edit, forward, copy, or save e-documents. The rights can even be controlled by time of day (e.g. access during work hours only) or type of device (e.g. access on the PC but not mobile devices). Rights are assigned upon creation of the document, usually according to roles (levels) in the organization. These access rights travel with the e-document itself, and access can be turned off remotely (via the Cloud or a server) if an employee has had their laptop or computing device compromised or stolen, or if the employee has been terminated. So even if an organization like Anthem Health were hacked and completely compromised, ePHI, ePII, and confidential documents would still be protected, in an encrypted state. Or if a rogue hacker or internal bad actor accesses thousands of electronic health records, they

would not be viewable and could not be copied or printed. Certainly, technologies in this category are a part of supporting an IG program.

2. **Data loss prevention (DLP)** – Software that continuously monitors and thoroughly inspects information that flows (e.g. e-mail, e-documents) on a network and attempts to prevent ePHI, ePII, or certain sensitive information containing certain key words or phrases from exiting the organization past its firewall. DLP is often used in conjunction with IRM software and also to assist in data mapping efforts.

3. **Digital signatures** – Software that can break up business process bottlenecks that can occur for authorizations/approvals. Digital signatures carry detailed audit information used to detect unauthorized modifications to e-documents and to authenticate the identity of the signatory (in a process known as non-repudiation).

4. **Database activity monitoring (DAM)** and database auditing tools monitor databases in real time for anomalies and unusual activity and create an audit trail generated in real time that can be the forensic smoking gun when attacks have occurred.

5. **Print security** – To help secure large print files—which contain highly useful information for hackers as the information is distilled and in one place—specialized hardware devices designed to sit between the print server and the network "cloak" print files and they are only visible to those who have a properly configured cloaking device on the other end.

6. **Security vulnerability/penetration testing software** – Software in this category allows organizations to test and find any security vulnerabilities they may have, and to address these weaknesses through security patches and other methods;

7. **Stream messaging** – For confidential communications, this approach leaves no record of an e-mail exchange; that is, once the e-mail message is read, it "vaporizes" completely. This prevents printing, forwarding or altering the message.

Next, information technologies that assist in the "Control" of information (and, of course there is some overlap with Security):

1. **Electronic Health Record (EHR)** – Software to capture and track the record of diagnosis and treatment of a patient. Contains both clinical data and unstructured output such as dictated history and physical, narrative notes, diagrams (e.g. EKG), images (e.g. x-ray, CAT), and other information related to patient care.

2. **Identity and Access Management (IAM)** controls logon credentials, and aims to prevent unauthorized access. IAM governs access to information through an automated, continuous process. Implemented properly, IAM keeps access limited to authorized users.

3. **Document analytics** – This type of software monitors access, use, and printing of e-documents in real time. Graphical reports are created—so if a user normally downloads or prints 10 documents a day, and on one day they download or print 1,000 or 10,000—red flags go off.

4. **Document labeling** is the process of attaching a label to classify a document, which is a simple way to increase user awareness about the sensitivity of a document—for instance, by labeling it "confidential."

5. **Business Process Management Suites (BPMS)** – This software allows organizations to control business processes and to model and simulate business process routing and processing options to automate a process from end to end. The ability to make intelligent changes in process based on metrics and real-time feedback facilitates optimization of the efficiency of business processes.

6. **Enterprise Content Management (ECM)** to manage all types of unstructured content. ECM controls access and manages versions of e-documents, web pages, reports and other digital assets. ECM is being somewhat displaced by cloud-based **Enterprise File Synch and Share (EFSS)** platforms such as Box and Dropbox.

7. **Mobile Device Management (MDM)** to manage and control the network of mobile devices. MDM allows an organization to update mobile devices en masse with security patches and updates, to remotely wipe lost or stolen devices of confidential data, and to monitor the mobile network.[2]

Lastly, technologies that assist in the "Optimization" of information:

1. **File analysis, classification, and remediation (FACR)** – Software tools in this category scan the entire collection of information (e.g. e-documents) across shared drives, storage area networks, and all other storage devices to conduct "file analysis." File analysis can scan and find metadata such as author, topic, file type, date of creation, date of last access, etc. This process can help the healthcare organization to locate where personal confidential information like ePII, ePHI, and ePCI is stored so it may be protected with encryption, and also to dispose of it as is legally required. Further, the more sophisticated tools can actually begin to insert classification metadata tags to help organize the content and to assist in the remediation process, which includes deleting duplicates and "data debris," which no longer has business value to the organization.

2. **Advanced Data Analytics** – Software with the capability far beyond traditional business intelligence (BI).[3] Categorized as **descriptive analytics** ("what happened"), **diagnostic analytics** (comparing historical data to determine "why" some events occurred – e.g. "a healthcare provider compares patients' response to a promotional campaign in different regions")[4], **predictive analytics** ("what might happen"), and **prescriptive analytics** ("what we should do to exploit a promising trend or head off a looming problem"). Advanced analytics can process and analyze thousands or even millions of data points to help harvest new clinical insights and make predictions/recommendations that can help in improving patient outcomes and patient satisfaction, as well as find innovations to improve operational efficiency and financial performance.

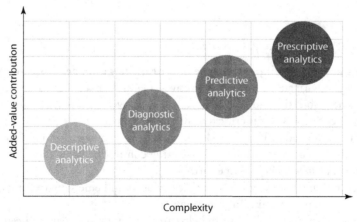

3. **Predictive coding** – During the early case assessment (ECA) phase of the e-discovery legal process, predictive coding is a "court endorsed process" that can be utilized for document

review. Legal experts review a subset of documents and "teach" the software which documents are responsive in a particular legal matter, and the software goes through a sorting and sifting process to find similar documents. This is an iterative process where the human legal expert continues to review a sampling of the documents found by the software to provide input and facilitate improved accuracy by the software in finding responsive documents. The result is *drastically reduced costs for document review*, which can be accomplished in a much shorter timeframe giving legal teams more insights and more time to develop strategy. When applied to business data, predictive analytics can also help you to find new insights and trends to act upon, perhaps to improve operational efficiency, cross-sell customers, or even to develop new products and services. In healthcare, leveraging predictive coding technology can go further and assist caregivers in anticipating patient needs, and can assist researchers in finding patterns and new insights to develop new treatment regimens.

4. **Business intelligence (BI)** uses software tools and techniques to analyze raw (structured) data to help provide useful insights for managers and executives to make more informed decisions. New insights into the data can be gleaned, which can help spur innovation in marketing, product and patient services development, finance, and other key business areas.

5. **Content analytics (CA)** software applies BI and business analytics to better gain insights into content volumes and patterns, and how the content may be used. CA can help improve findability of websites, brands, and products;

6. **Master data management (MDM)** – This type of software helps organizations to perform data governance and data quality functions, which are key to IG efforts not only in the IT department but also in maintaining patient records with high quality data. The goal of MDM software is to ensure that accurate, reliable data from a single source is leveraged across business units. That is, the key aim is to establish "a single version of the truth" and eliminate multiple, inconsistent versions of data sets. Downstream reports which rely on this data are therefore more accurate and trusted by managers;

With just the above examples, it is *quite clear* that there are a number of technology tools which can be leveraged to address various aspects and aims of IG programs.

Chapter Summary: Key Points

■ **An IG framework (IGF) provides the guardrails to guide decisions in the IG program.**
■ An IGF begins with stated business objectives. Begin IG planning with a focus on organizational business objectives and be sure that IG objectives are aligned to support them.
■ A strong executive sponsor is critical to IG program success.
■ The IG Program Lead or Program Manager (PM) plays a key role in managing the relationship with the executive sponsor and IG steering committee.
■ IG requires a *change management* effort.
■ There are a number of key information technologies and emerging technologies that help to secure, control, and optimize information.
■ Advanced analytics technologies can help caregivers anticipate patient needs, improve treatment regimens and patient outcomes, and even improve marketing effectiveness.

Notes

1. Linda Kloss, *Implementing Health Information Governance: Lessons from the Field* (AHIMA Press, 2015), p. 10.
2. "Mobile Communications and Records and Information Management," ARMA technical report TR-20-2012, ARMA International, August 2012.
3. "Advanced Analytics," Gartner IT Glossary, https://www.gartner.com/it-glossary/advanced-analytics.
4. Aliaksander Bekker, "4 Types of Data Analytics to Improve Decision-Making," ScienceSoft, July 11, 2017, https://www.scnsoft.com/blog/4-types-of-data-analytics.

Chapter 6

Getting Started: Where to Launch an IG Program

7 Key IG Accelerators to Launch an IG Program

One of biggest problems with kicking off new IG programs is that, on average, they take a year or more to form, according to industry research. Beyond that, many IG programs lose steam and fail to meet the organization's objectives. This can occur for a variety of reasons, adhering to the Anna Karenina principle, which derives from the opening to Tolstoy's book:

> "Happy families are all alike; every unhappy family is unhappy in its own way."

That is to say, every IG program failure is unique and due to a varying mix of shortcomings.

One IG industry leader confided, "I have designed perfect IG programs and nothing happened." In this case, there likely were significant weaknesses in the approach, including lack of strong executive sponsorship and developing a clear business case.

Other failed IG programs may not have had the right combination of players named to the IG steering committee, or it was overstaffed and not tiered so it got bogged down. Others may not have properly planned roles and a clear **Responsibility Assignment Matrix**, or RACI matrix (which identifies those **R**esponsible, **A**ccountable, **C**onsulted, and **I**nformed) early on, which doomed the program to failure. Still others may have lost focus on the organizational change management and communications aspects that are required to keep an IG program on track.

Responsible IG Lead	Accountable Executive Sponsor
Consulted Key Stakeholders and SMEs	Informed Board of Directors, Broader Stakeholder Group

But there have been some lessons learned from these failures, and the approaches to creating and maintaining successful IG programs are starting to coalesce.

Here are seven key accelerators which can help launch or expand a successful IG program:

1. **Recruit a strong executive sponsor**. As noted in previous sections of this book, recruiting a strong executive sponsor is paramount. If there are multiple executive sponsors on board then nominate the most senior one (and consider making one or more of the others deputy sponsors). If that is not logical, select the executive with the most engagement and commitment, and the most to lose or gain. When evaluating executive sponsors, find that manager who has the highest information risk levels, the one who has the most to lose from a data breach, from non-compliance fines, or from soaring legal costs. Or that has a department full of knowledge workers who cannot find the information they need on a timely basis, consistently. Or even a department with rapidly increasing information storage costs. Think CFO, General Counsel, CIO, COO, Chief Risk Officer, Chief Information Security Officer, Chief Privacy Officer, and similar titles. (Ideally, the CEO or Administrator would be a solid choice due to their seniority.) C-level executives have clear budget and decision authority. These senior executives likely have been considering various piecemeal measures and it is the IG program lead's job to educate them on the benefits of taking a holistic IG approach and aligning the effort with strategic business objectives.[1]

2. **Find common ground**. It is recommended that the IG Lead form alliances to help bolster the IG program effort. There are several groups that can be natural allies, but, of course, the scenario depends on business objectives, office politics, budget availability, and other organizational factors. Data governance is one of the first places to look. Most larger healthcare organizations have some form of a data governance program or at least data quality program that operates on an ongoing basis. Some healthcare organizations have a chief data officer (CDO) dedicated to this function. The goals of a data governance program align with higher level IG program goals, especially the noble pursuit of improving patient outcomes and saving lives. There are a plethora of benefits that flow from a rigid data governance program related to improving patient outcomes, such as improving patient trust, satisfaction, and loyalty; reducing litigation rates and costs; improving operational efficiency; and, increasing organizational value. Remember, *IG programs must be driven from the top down, but implemented from the bottom up for best results.* So an alliance with the CDO or data governance program manager should be a good alliance. Find these types of natural business allies to gain momentum in the IG effort. If the IG program lead comes from the HIM area, their skills can be helpful in working with the CDO to improve the accuracy of clinical data that is generated form lab and diagnostic equipment that is stored in the EHR. The HIM manager can also work with General Counsel to improve litigation readiness, reduce legal e-discovery costs, and reduce attorney document review costs. If the IG program lead comes from IT, they may need to team with the HIM lead and approach business unit leaders who have the biggest information management problems or the most litigation and help them improve their approach to records and e-document management. If the Business Office is planning to implement real-time e-mail archiving, and the e-mail policy is going to have to be reviewed and revised, this is a good time to dovetail off that project to launch or expand the IG effort.

3. **Leverage assessment or audit findings**. An internal assessment or audit of procedures and practices may reveal weaknesses that are putting organizational information at risk. One assessment tool with strengths in assessing healthcare organizations is AHIMA's IG*HealthRate*™, a purpose-built assessment and measurement platform for IG which has the Information

Governance Adoption Model™ embedded in it. Another more comprehensive and mature IG assessment tool to use is the **Information Governance Process Maturity Model** from CGOC.org, which measures maturity on 22 key IG processes.[2] If evaluating specific aspects of an IG program, such as cyber-security, the ISO 27001/2 standards can be used as guidelines. Findings from an internal assessment can provide the mandate for moving forward with an IG program.[3]

4. **Piggyback on existing IT projects**, especially those that are approved and funded, or those that are likely to be. For instance, if the organization is planning on migrating installed EHR software to a new vendor, this is a good time to focus on getting good, clean, quality data into that new system, by working closely with the data governance team. If there is a Chief Data Officer and robust data governance program, IG is a natural fit. If, in another instance, the business side of the organization is due for a refresh in enterprise content management (ECM) software, or it is cleaning up shared drives and/or migrating to SharePoint, this would be an ideal time to go a step further and implement a more comprehensive IG program that can work in lockstep with the ECM implementation. If legal hold notification (LHN) has been implemented and now additional efficiencies in the e-discovery process are being pursued, a broader IG approach may be well-timed.[4]

5. **Emphasize hard cost savings**. Where can hard dollar savings be found? When looking for a hard dollar benefit, an easy target is data storage and shrinking the storage footprint. Typically, 40% or more of information that healthcare organizations store has no business value. With a current and complete data map and leveraging file analysis tools using file analysis software, it can be graphically demonstrated to executives which information is worthless—redundant, outdated, or trivial (ROT)—and how much storage costs could be cut or at least the rate of growth can be slowed. Then layer on the benefits of improved clinical analysis and patient care capabilities, information risk reduction, reputational risk reduction, improved compliance capabilities, improved productivity, and improved efficiency in implementing legal holds and other litigation-related tasks. Other cost impact areas may be reductions in cyber-insurance costs and e-discovery costs due to an ongoing IG program.[5]

6. **Cite the impact of poor IG**. In launching an IG program, often citing the "worst case" scenario will help make the case. One approach is to provide some well-known examples of breaches of ePHI or ePII that have heavily damaged companies like Premera BlueCross, Excellus BlueCross BlueShield,[6] Anthem Health,[7] and 21st Century Oncology. Be sure to delineate the fallout from these breaches to make the case for the IG program. When considering the impact of a ransomware attack, bear in mind that over two-thirds of U.S. consumers would consider changing providers if their provider were attacked by ransomware, according to a recent survey.[8] Another approach could be to list major HIPAA fines that peer organizations have paid when making the case for moving forward with an IG program.

7. **Establishing a legal defense**. If executives still are not convinced, then communicate to them that in cases like Excellus and Anthem, where patients or employees have had their personal data compromised, there will be lawsuits. Lots of lawsuits. And if an organization has an IG program in place and has taken reasonable "best effort" steps—basic measures such as information security awareness training—to secure private information including ePII and ePHI, and sensitive information like race or religion, then the foundation for a legal defense is in place. Although culpability may possibly be found, the awards will be smaller which lowers the cost of legal claims.[9]

These are some of the accelerators that can help get an IG program launched or expanded.

Chapter Summary: Key Points

- **IG programs fail for a variety of reasons.**
- Piggyback on existing, funded IT projects such as a move to a new electronic health record (EHR) system or an existing data governance program to help launch the IG program.
- IG programs must be driven from the top down, and implemented from the bottom up.
- A strong executive sponsor is crucial.
- Find natural internal allies to launch an IG effort—those who have the most to gain from IG.
- Findings from an internal audit can provide the mandate for moving forward with an IG program.
- Show hard dollar savings, and then add the benefits of information risk reduction to justify IG.
- Cite the "worst case" impact of poor IG (e.g. major breaches, fines) when making the business case to move forward.
- An IG program in place means management has taken reasonable "best effort" steps to secure PHI and PII, which can help a future legal defense.

Notes

1. Barclay T. Blair, "Information Governance: 10 Things You Can Do To Get Started," online webinar, Zylab, July 23, 2014, http://www.zylab.com/ediscovery-resources/recorded-webcasts.
2. "2017 CGOC Information Governance Process Maturity Model," CGOC, https://www.cgoc.com/resource/information-governance-process-maturity-model.
3. Craig Callé, "Why Data Needs a Seat at the Corporate Table," CFO, December 9, 2015, http://ww2.cfo.com/big-data-tecnology/2015/12/why-data-needs-a-seat-at-the-corporate-table-information-governance.
4. Barclay T. Blair, "Information Governance: 10 Things You Can Do To Get Started," online webinar, Zylab, July 23, 2014, http://www.zylab.com/ediscovery-resources/recorded-webcasts.
5. Ibid.
6. Jessica Davis, "7 Largest Data Breaches of 2015," Healthcare IT News, December 11, 2015, http://www.healthcareitnews.com/news/7-largest-data-breaches-2015.
7. Cameron F. Kerry, "Lessons from the New Threat Environment from Sony, Anthem and ISIS." Brookings Institution, March 26, 2015, http://www.brookings.edu/blogs/techtank/posts/2015/03/26-anthem-sony-isis-hack-cybersecurity.
8. Rebecca Wynn, CISSP, CRISC, CASP, CCISO, LinkedIn post, May 31, 2017.
9. "The Principles," ARMA International, 2009, http://w2.arma.org/r2/generally-accepted-br-recordkeeping-principles.

Chapter 7

Making the Business Case to Justify an IG Program

The best way to measure the viability of an IG program is by determining if the investment of time and resources is going to be a worthwhile and profitable one.

The first step in justifying an IG program is to understand what key factors qualify a project as viable in a particular organization. Once that is known, steps to build the business case that satisfy or exceed those requirements can be taken.

Look for hard cost savings first. Beyond that, the benefits of information risk reduction, lower rates of medical mistakes, reduced legal exposure, and productivity of knowledge workers must be made clear to executive management to help solidify the business case.

At times the business rationale for implementing an IG program may begin with qualitative analysis; however, efforts to improve qualitatively can turn into measurable quantitative gains. For instance, focusing on patient satisfaction can bring real improvements in patient outcomes which are reflected in improved population health and reduced mortality rates.

The executive sponsor must actively develop and *own* the business case, so it is important to get it right. It is best to look for hard dollar savings where possible, establish meaningful metrics, and attempt to quantify the value of ongoing information risk reduction. That value can be realized in actual financial savings when negotiating cyber-insurance rates. It can also be measured as a cost avoidance value when breaches are avoided, suppressed, or their damage is minimized.

There are clear tangible and intangible benefits to implementing IG, and multiple business drivers to justify an IG program. Improving patient outcomes and reducing mortality rates are paramount goals, followed by the impact of possible leakage of ePHI and ePII, fears of HIPAA compliance violations and major fines, spiraling e-discovery costs, or even **European General Data Protection Regulation** (GDPR) non-compliance.

Why Healthcare Organizations Are at the Greatest Risk

When rogue players go after healthcare institutions, they do so because not only can they gain access to financial information, but also to insurance credentials and patient health histories.

This information lasts a lifetime and hackers can sell it on the **dark web** for much more than basic credit card information, which becomes obsolete once passwords are changed. Further, the health record and insurance credentials can be sold and people can use these stolen credentials to have expensive medical procedures performed. They simply have to be the same gender and blood type, and approximately the same age and race, and then with these stolen health credentials they may have a hip or shoulder replaced, or perhaps even heart surgery.

A 2017 study by the Ponemon Institute[1] showed that healthcare data breaches were the most costly of all industry sectors, outpacing most sectors by a factor of two to one.

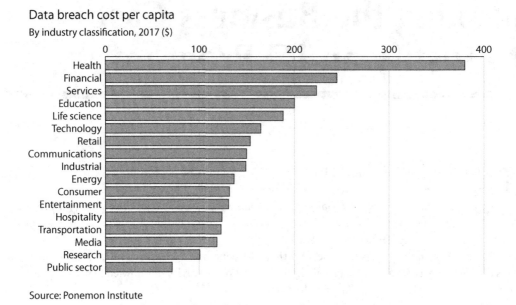

Data breach cost per capita
By industry classification, 2017 ($)

Source: Ponemon Institute

Saving Lives: Improving Patient Care and Outcomes

It is clear that the leading goal of IG programs in healthcare is to improve clinical outcomes, save lives, and improve overall population health. With this as a driving program focus, there are several aspects that can be addressed. First, a robust data governance program focusing on improving clinical data quality can help improve the accuracy of provider analyses, improve care, and improve patient outcomes. It can also provide more accurate data for longitudinal studies. Second, a program focus can emphasize reducing medical mistakes, which are the third leading cause of death in the U.S. behind heart disease and cancer, killing over a quarter of a million Americans each year.[2] Third, the use of analytics can not only improve the quality of analysis for caregivers to base their decisions upon, thereby improving patient outcomes, but also, there can be broader benefits. For instance, software developed at Boston Children's Hospital uses analytics to detect "subtle patterns" and "faint signals" in detecting, plotting, and tracking disease outbreaks.[3] The software, HealthMap, scans "billions of posts from tens of thousands of social media sites, local news, government publications, infectious-disease online physicians' discussion groups, RSS feeds, and other sources." This process is repeated hourly to keep it current. It also uses **machine learning** technology (a form of **artificial intelligence**) to improve its prediction capabilities by matching confirmed disease outbreaks with information that had been compiled on them. The ability to quickly identify outbreaks can assist local healthcare organizations to respond and contain them more quickly and effectively.

Population Health Milestones and Metrics

Each organization will have a different set of milestones and metrics to measure progress. Some sample ones that can be used in the population health area of your IG program include:

1. Implement new medical error detection procedures and audit checks within six months.
2. Reduce medical mistakes by 10% from the average for the previous five years (or national average), within two years.
3. Reduce mortality rates for specific conditions (e.g. breast cancer) by 5% within three years.
4. Improve patient satisfaction rates by 20% over a baseline measurement within two years.

Breach and Ransomware Preparedness and Patient Trust

Information security is one of the main pillars of IG. Safeguarding patient records is of paramount importance. Consumers expect healthcare organizations not only to care for them, but also to exercise care and prudence when handling their PHI and sensitive data.

Breaches in the healthcare industry have become increasingly common. Some of the major data breaches in 2017 included:

■ Potentially over 100,000 patients' ePHI was breached at **Mid-Michigan Physicians Imaging Center**, although only seven were confirmed. The Center delayed reporting the breach while they investigated, and ended up paying a $475,000 fine levied by the Health and Human Services Office for Civil Rights (OCR), as timely reporting is required for HIPAA compliance.

■ Bupa, an international health insurer, reported that an employee stole the PII of over 100,000 customers, but that the majority of their over 1.4 million customers were not affected. Since the theft, Bupa has increased security measures and conducted an investigation.

■ Washington State University reported the theft of a locked safe which contained a hard drive holding the personal data of about one million people.

■ Molina Healthcare, a major Medicaid and Affordable Care Act insurer, shut down its patient portal after it found a rudimentary security flaw allowing access to patient medical claims data. Over 4.8 million patient accounts may have been affected.

Also in 2017, OCR levied a civil penalty of $3.2 million against Children's Medical Center of Dallas for breaches of ePHI which occurred in 2009 and 2013.[4]

A major data breach creates a breach of patient trust, and this can have financial consequences for healthcare organizations. *Over two-thirds of consumers stated they would consider leaving their healthcare provider if it suffered a ransomware attack.*[5]

Ransomware attacks were classified as breaches in a July 2016 statement by the Health and Human Services Office for Civil Rights (OCR). The OCR went further and stated that ransomware attacks are subject to the HIPAA Breach Notification Rule.

In April 2017, a ransomware attack was made on 6,000 computers at Erie County Medical Center (ECMC) in Buffalo, New York.[6] Short ransom notes began popping up on staff computer screens saying the hospital's files had been encrypted, along with a demand for payment of approximately $30,000 in bitcoins. ECMC shut down its computer systems within 90 minutes and began operating offline. They were determined not to pay the ransom, and they did not. But it was very costly. The disruption lasted over six weeks and cost ECMC nearly $10 million, as they wiped all computers completely clean of any data and restored them from backups. During most of that time patient registration, notes, and prescriptions were written by hand and for the first three weeks lab results were sent by couriers. Should they have just paid the $30,000? Hindsight is 20/20, but management may have been fearful that even if they paid, the ransom requests would continue, and could escalate, and that there still could be malware lurking on their systems. They took a prudent, yet expensive, course. But if they had had an IG program implemented, the attack may have never taken place. Hackers, like robbers, go for the easiest and most vulnerable targets.

Other management teams have decided to pay the ransom, report it, and then focus on hardening their information security practices and training employees on emerging threats. In February 2016, Hollywood Presbyterian Medical Center paid $17,000 worth of bitcoins in ransom to regain access to their systems which had been encrypted.[7]

Another ransomware attack took place in June 2017, hitting Pacific Alliance Medical Center (PAMC) in Los Angeles and compromising the ePHI and other sensitive data of over 260,000 patients.[8] PAMC's notice to patients did not state whether or not ransom was paid, but officials could not rule out whether the ePHI was viewed or stolen.

Due to the July 2016 statement made by the Office for Civil Rights, tightening its reporting requirements for ransomware, PAMC took a cautious approach to reporting the incident and also offered two years of identity theft monitoring to its patients at no cost.[9]

Other Types of Breaches: Medical Devices

Connected medical devices offer new possibilities for continuously monitored patient care, which can improve outcomes and research data collection. In the U.S., an average of 10–15 devices are connected per hospital bed. With more and more medical devices being connected, there are inherent vulnerabilities that bad actors may exploit. For instance, in September 2017, the Department of Homeland Security warned that a security flaw in syringe infusion pumps made by Smith Medical may allow hackers to gain access and control of the device, even changing the amount and timing of medication that is administered.[10]

So healthcare organizations must, as a part of their overall IG program, institute a thorough medical device connectivity vulnerability evaluation program, beginning with vetting vendors and changing default security settings. (Smith Medical issued a software patch to address the vulnerability and stated the issue was resolved in January 2018.)

Cyber-security Milestones and Metrics

Some basic milestones and metrics that can be used in the cyber-security area of your IG program include:

1. Security Awareness Training: Train all information-handling employees on cyber-security hygiene within 90 days, and measure their retention with basic testing.

2. Create an ongoing communications and training plan for cyber-security hygiene and implement within 90 days.
3. Complete a mock breach response exercise, analyze any weaknesses, and update procedures within 90 days.
4. Reduce the number of lost or stolen mobile devices by 50% over the previous year.
5. Reduce hacker intrusion events by 25% over the previous year.

Safeguarding Privacy

Information security is the first requirement before information privacy can be enforced in an IG program. Patient privacy is part of the trust equation consumers have with healthcare providers. Special privacy protections for health information go back centuries. The Hippocratic Oath states, "I will respect the privacy of my patients, for their problems are not disclosed to me that the world may know."[11] The doctor–patient relationship is protected in many countries by not only tradition, but law.

To ensure patient privacy is vigilantly guarded, a fundamental step is to initiate **privacy awareness training** as a part of an overall IG program. This training can include a review and update on patient privacy rights, information on the latest phishing, smishing (using SMS text), and ransomware attacks. Also the training could review privacy guidelines for the use of e-mail, mobile devices, cloud applications, and social media.

Information Privacy Milestones and Metrics

Some basic milestones and metrics that can be used in the information privacy area of your IG program include:

1. Privacy Awareness Training: Train 50% of information-handling employees on information privacy laws and Best Practices within 45 days, the remaining 50% within 90 days, and measure their retention with basic testing.
2. Create an ongoing communications and training plan for patient privacy and implement within 90 days. Reach 100% of the target employees within 90 days.
3. Update the organizational privacy policy within 90 days and publish on corporate website, and brief 100% of employees in the target group within 90 days.
4. Complete a mock privacy breach response tabletop exercise, analyze any weaknesses, and update procedures within 90 days.

Improving Operational Efficiency

Legally defensible deletion of information, that is, deletion based on standardized, enforced policies, is going to be a driver of cost reduction in any IG program. The goal of these efforts is to shrink the "storage footprint"—the gross amount of information being stored by the organization—and therefore reduce operating costs. In addition, this process has other benefits.

Deleting **redundant, outdated, and trivial** (ROT) business information—which is approximately 40%–70% of what the majority of organizations manage—will not only drive down hard storage costs, but it also helps to reduce legal and compliance risks and make information more findable and accessible for knowledge workers, boosting their productivity while improving the professional work environment.

Operational Efficiency Milestones and Metrics

Some basic milestones and metrics that can be used in the operational efficiency/productivity area of your IG program include:

1. Train knowledge workers in the target areas on new search capabilities and methods within 90 days.
2. Reduce average time spent searching for information by knowledge workers in the Business Office by 25% over previous baseline results, within one year.
3. Use file analysis software to conduct a cleanup and cut ROT on shared drives from a baseline of approximately 40% to 20% or less within one year.
4. Use file analysis software to conduct a cleanup and reduce storage footprint of shared drives in business units by 20% within six months.

Reducing Legal Costs

Electronic information is being created today at unprecedented and increasing rates. Healthcare organizations, which have typically been laggards in technology implementations when compared to other industry segments, are struggling to manage this onslaught, and it is driving up legal costs. "This surplus of electronically stored information (ESI) is, in reality, driving up the cost of storage, raising the cost and risk of eDiscovery and regulatory compliance, negatively impacting employee productivity, and raising the prospect of intellectual property theft and ePII leakage."[12]

A robust IG program addresses these growing challenges.

Critical questions to raise during the decision-making process include: *What if we are not able to meet legal demands for records production during litigation? What can happen if auditors or regulators investigated our recordkeeping practices?* These types of serious questions must be asked and can only be addressed with a successful IG program.

Legal Operations Milestones and Metrics

Some basic milestones and metrics that can be used in the Legal area of your IG program include:

1. Revise and update the Legal Hold Notification (LHN) process within six months.
2. Train all data stewards and business unit heads on new LHN within nine months.
3. Evaluate, select, and implement predictive coding software within six months, and train 10 power users.
4. Reduce the cost-per-GB for attorney review of e-documents from a baseline of approximately $18K/GB to $10K/GB or less within one year.
5. Use file analysis software to conduct a cleanup and cut ROT on shared drives from a baseline of approximately 40% to 20% or less within one year.
6. Evaluate, select and implement digital signature software within six months, and train 10 power users.

One Big Negative Event Can Change the Ballgame

The September 11th terrorist attacks on New York and Washington, D.C., and Hurricane Katrina hitting New Orleans and the Gulf Coast changed the realities of disaster recovery and business continuity plans. And the WikiLeaks revelations changed the realities of e-document security. So too can one large adverse event—like a major data breach or particularly costly lawsuit—change the way a healthcare organization considers managing, securing, and governing information.

Business Drivers for IG Programs

According to Osterman Research, in its report entitled, *The True ROI of Information Governance*, the top three drivers for justifying an IG program are:

1. Risk avoidance;
2. Regulatory risk mitigation; and,
3. Employee productivity improvement.[13]

As noted in that report, having a comprehensive understanding of total costs before and after applying any solutions is the key to building a believable ROI Model. The cost analysis might focus in a target area and may be as simple as information storage costs, or more complex and somewhat of a moving target like e-discovery collection and review costs. (Often it is tough to get an internal legal team to break these out accurately.)

Once the baseline costs have been determined, estimated savings can be calculated using the appropriate financial models or justification approaches that suit a particular organization.

Hard Cost Savings

1. **Information collection during litigation**: As the volume and velocity of electronically stored information (ESI) rises, so will e-discovery costs during litigation rise, and the costs and effort to classify, categorize, and manage ESI on a daily basis. End users will take the path of least resistance, which means the information will be organized in accordance with the skillset of those end users, and with a minimum of effort. The lack of consistency will ultimately add to information collection costs whenever there is an e-discovery request.[14]
2. **Document review for litigation**: This function is usually done by attorneys or high-end paralegals at an hourly billing rate per document or per megabyte. The more documents subject to legal review, the higher the cost. By proactively removing unnecessary and irrelevant ESI, fewer documents will have to be reviewed, resulting in lower review costs.
3. **Information storage savings**: Contrary to what many believe about storage costs getting cheaper, the exact opposite is true for organizations today (which rely on online access to enterprise storage), due to rapidly increasing volumes. One must consider the full cost of information ownership, which includes not only storage hardware but floor space, air conditioning, electricity to run the hardware and software, maintenance and support costs, staff salaries, contractor costs, and physical and software security, to name a few. As noted in the Osterman report, "an IG program will deliver two areas of storage savings: the percentage of storage

resources freed up due to more efficient and ongoing data retention/disposition procedures, and the continuing storage savings from an ongoing defensible disposition practice."[15]

Soft Costs: Intangible Cost Offsets

There are also some less calculable benefits:

1. **Potential revenue gains**: Often overlooked is the gain in revenue as a result of recovered employee productivity. When employees in, say, the Business Office spend fewer hours searching for and/or re-creating information, they spend more time engaged in activities that could generate more revenue for the organization (such as billing and collections). That enhanced productivity can generate real top-line revenue growth.[16] In addition, performing analytics on cleaned data can provide new insights that may result in new revenue-generating product and service innovations.

2. **Information risk reduction**: Risk avoidance involves taking steps to mitigate exposure to negative events. Risk mitigation is a key component and goal of IG programs. An organization's business risk impact from IG may take the form of reducing the likelihood of lawsuits by reducing medical mistakes, or reducing the likelihood of a breach or ransomware attack. It can also improve the odds of winning lawsuits due to more efficient collection and review of responsive information, giving the legal team more time and resources to spend on a winning strategy. At the same time the organization will be lowering its risk of compliance violations of HIPAA and other major regulations, reducing the likelihood of court sanctions and fines, which can be substantial and run into the millions. Further, the organization is improving its information security defenses, guarding against breaches and protecting the brand while reducing exposure to reputational risk.[17]

3. **Improvements in knowledge worker productivity**: When an organization's highest-paid professionals cannot locate information to make a decision, they must waste time searching and may ultimately end up doing double-work by re-creating the information. This is difficult to calculate, but it is a real cost. An average knowledge worker can spend 15%–25% of their workweek simply *searching* for information, according to studies. The organization should shoot for providing the *right* information to the *right* professionals at the *right* time— *securely.* When this is the aim of an IG program, substantial productivity benefits will accrue and management will be promoting a more professional and efficient work environment, while minimizing staffing needs.

It is clear that an overarching IG program can yield many benefits to healthcare organizations, through a series of discrete projects aimed at reducing information risk while improving information quality, safety, privacy, and value. In the near future, Information Asset Valuation (IAV) software will be available to aid executives and IG Program Managers in calculating the true financial costs and benefits of an IG program.

Chapter Summary: Key Points

- **The executive sponsor must develop and *own* the business case.**
- Healthcare information is target-rich for hackers. Insurance credentials and patient health histories are very valuable.

- Improving patient outcomes and reducing mortality are key goals of IG programs in healthcare.
- A major data breach creates a breach of patient trust, and this can have financial consequences for healthcare organizations.
- OCR classified ransomware attacks as breaches in 2016, and they are now subject to the HIPAA Breach Notification Rule.
- Connected medical devices mean new vulnerabilities to patient data that must be addressed.
- A privacy awareness training program can help educate employees on being cautious with patient information.
- Legally defensible deletion of information is a key driver of cost reduction in IG programs as it can reduce the storage footprint and electronic storage costs.
- One major data breach or costly lawsuit can provide the justification for an IG program.
- Major hard dollar savings in the Legal area come from e-discovery collection and document review cost reductions.
- There may be additional opportunities for revenue growth by using analytics to process data in the IG program effort.
- Risk mitigation is a key component and goal of IG programs.
- Information Governance programs produce substantial productivity benefits which accrue from cleaner, more accessible information.

Notes

1. Jessica Twentyman, "Hacking Medical Devices is the Next Big Security Concern," *Financial Times*, November 8, 2017, https://www.ft.com/content/75912040-98ad-11e7-8c5c-c8d8fa6961bb?segmentid=acee4131-99c2-09d3-a635-873e61754ec6.
2. Dan Munro, "U.S. Healthcare Ranked Dead Last Compared to 10 Other Countries," Forbes.com, June 16, 2014, http://www.forbes.com/sites/danmunro/2014/06/16/u-s-healthcare-ranked-dead-last-compared-to-10-other-countries/#7aa717021b96.
3. Doug Laney, *Infonomics: How to Monetize, Manage, and Measure Information as an Asset for Competitive Advantage* (Bibliomotion, 2017), pp. 95–96.
4. "Lack of Timely Action Risks Security and Costs Money," U.S. Department of Health and Human Services, February 1, 2017, https://www.hhs.gov/about/news/2017/02/01/lack-timely-action-risks-security-and-costs-money.html.
5. "Survey: Many US Consumers Would Leave Provider over Ransomware Attack," SmartBrief.com, May 30, 2017, http://www.smartbrief.com/s/2017/05/survey-many-us-consumers-would-leave-provider-over-ransomware-attack.
6. Jonathan Crowe, "How One Ransomware Attack Cost Erie County Medical Center $10 Million," Barkly.com, August 2017, https://blog.barkly.com/10-million-dollar-ecmc-hospital-ransomware-attack.
7. Richard Winton, "Hollywood Hospital Pays $17,000 in Bitcoin to Hackers; FBI Investigating," *Los Angeles Times*, February 18, 2016, http://beta.latimes.com/business/technology/la-me-ln-hollywood-hospital-bitcoin-20160217-story.html.
8. Jessica Davis, "Los Angeles Provider Breached by Ransomware Attack, over 260,000 Patients Affected (UPDATED)," Healthcare IT News, August 14, 2017, http://www.healthcareitnews.com/news/los-angeles-provider-breached-ransomware-attack-over-260000-patients-affected-updated.
9. Ibid.
10. Jessican Twentyman, "Hacking Medical Devices is the Next Big Security Concern," *Financial Times*, November 8, 2017, https://www.ft.com/content/75912040-98ad-11e7-8c5c-c8d8fa6961bb?segmentid=acee4131-99c2-09d3-a635-873e61754ec6.
11. Peter P. Swire, Kenesa Ahmad, *Foundations of Information Privacy and Data Protection* (IAPP, 2012), p. 67.

12. "The True ROI of Information Governance," Osterman Research white paper, February, 2015, p. 1.
13. Ibid, p. 5.
14. Ibid, p. 10.
15. Ibid, p. 11.
16. Ibid, p. 11.
17. Ibid, p. 11.

Chapter 8

Information Risk Planning and Management

Information risk planning is a key Information Governance (IG) program activity. In health-care organizations, risk analysis is a HIPAA regulatory obligation as part of the administrative safeguard requirement.[1]

According to the Health and Human Services website, "Risk analysis should be an ongoing process, in which a covered entity [healthcare provider, plan, or clearinghouse] regularly reviews its records to track access to e-PHI and detect security incidents, periodically evaluates the effectiveness of security measures put in place, and regularly reevaluates potential risks to e-PHI."[2]

Often organizations have identified risks to information but have not taken the appropriate risk assessment and mitigation steps to counter those risks.

Information risk planning requires that the organization take a number of specific steps in identifying, analyzing, and countering information risks:

1. **Identify risks**. Conduct a formal process of identifying potential vulnerabilities and threats (both external and internal) to information assets.
2. **Assess impact**. Determine the potential financial and operational impact of the identified adverse events.
3. **Determine probability**. Weigh the likelihood that the identified risk events will materialize.
4. **Countermeasures**. Create high-level strategic plans to mitigate the greatest risks.
5. **Create policy**. Develop strategic plans into specific policies.
6. **Establish metrics**. Determine metrics to measure risk reductions from mitigation efforts.
7. **Assign responsibilities**. Identify those who are accountable for executing the new risk mitigating processes and maintaining the processes in place.
8. **Execute plan**. Execute the information risk mitigation plan.
9. **Audit, review, adjust**. Audit the information risk mitigation plan and make adjustments.

These risk mitigation efforts must be audited and tested periodically not only to ensure conformance to the policies, but also to provide a feedback loop to revise and fine-tune policies and optimize business processes.

Some key benefits to healthcare providers that flow from this information risk planning process include:

■ Protection and preservation of information assets;
■ Reduced deaths and injury due to medical mistakes;
■ Protection of the organization's reputation and brand;
■ Organizational "defense in depth" for privacy and security;
■ A direct connection to enterprise information security (cyber-security) practices which help to assure patient privacy;
■ Privacy controls that are clearly defined which reduce risks and support compliance efforts;
■ Privacy requirements that are measurable and enforceable;
■ Accountability in cyber-security and privacy processes.[3]

The Risk Planning Process

The risk planning steps, delineated in more detail, are:

Step 1: Conduct a Formal Process of Identifying Potential Vulnerabilities and Threats

Breaches. A key threat to all healthcare organizations is major data breaches. Breaches not only compromise patient ePHI but they also represent a breach of patient trust, which damages the institution's reputation. And it can be financially costly. Data breaches cost the healthcare industry $6.2 billion in 2016, according to the Ponemon Institute.[4]

In 2017, Metro Community Provider Network was fined $400,000 by the Office of Civil Rights (OCR) for overlooking risks that lead to a data breach. Other recent breaches include:

■ In 2017, Presence Health was fined $475,000 by OCR for lack of timely breach notification to patients.
■ Also in 2017, Centene, a multi-line healthcare enterprise, announced that nearly one million members may have been impacted by a data breach.[5] The breach was caused by the simple loss of hard drives that contained patient ePHI and PII.[6]
■ In 2016, St. Joseph's Health settled a class action lawsuit at a cost of $7.5 million for a 2012 data breach that affected over 30,000 of its patients. St. Joseph's was also fined $2.14 million by OCR in October 2016.[7]

HIPAA Violations. Another major risk facing healthcare institutions is HIPAA violations and the potential for large fines. These have not only immediate financial impact but also can erode the organization's reputation in the marketplace, which would impact future revenues and even shareholder equity value. There are many examples of major fines; below are a few recent examples (Table 8.1):

HIPAA and Business Associate Agreements

HIPAA regulations are often violated by not having business associate agreements in place, according to the OCR. A **business associate agreement** (BAA) is a standing contract between a

Table 8.1   Major HIPAA Fines in 2017

Date	Organization	Cause	Fine
January 2017	MAPFRE	HIPAA settlement demonstrates importance of implementing safeguards for ePHI	$2.2 M
February 2017	Children's Medical Center of Dallas	Lack of timely action risks security	$3.2 M
February 2017	Memorial Healthcare Systems	Lack of enforced audit controls	$5.5 M
April 2017	CardioNet	Lack of understanding of HIPAA requirements	$2.5 M
May 2017	Memorial Hermann Health System (MHHS)	PHI disclosure	$2.4 M

healthcare provider and third-party organizations providing services to that provider. The BAA is intended to safeguard PHI and patient privacy.[8]

Determining which contractors qualify as a HIPAA business associate can be challenging. Those who interact with or come in contact with PHI certainly qualify. In early 2016, the U.S. Department of Health and Human Services released guidance for software developers to assist in making the business associate determination.

Organizations typically underestimate the proliferation of PHI, or rather, ePHI. This is due to the fact that it is quite easy to duplicate electronic data, and most organizations are not actively using file analysis or data loss prevention (DLP) software to scan their electronic storage systems to locate incidences of PHI so it may be accounted for, tracked, and secured. This causes many healthcare organizations to be non-compliant with HIPAA requirements. Compounding this issue is the use of PHI in various departmental applications, and the increasing use of mobile devices, especially bring-your-own-device (BYOD).[9]

Ransomware. Ransomware is a newer type of risk that healthcare organizations face. Ransomware attacks typically occur when hackers intrude computer systems and lock down patient files with encryption, and then demand a fairly modest (although this has been increasing) ransom payment to unlock the files. Ransomware attacks were classified as breaches in a July 2016 statement by the Health and Human Services Office for Civil Rights (OCR). The OCR went further and stated that ransomware attacks are subject to the HIPAA Breach Notification Rule.

Ransomware attacks on healthcare institutions continue to increase and become more aggressive. According to the Verizon 2017 Data Breach Report, more than two-thirds (72%) of malware attacks in the healthcare industry were caused by ransomware.[10] A report by Symantec supported Verizon's findings, stating that in 2016 alone, ransomware attacks increased by 36% in healthcare.

Perhaps the most widespread ransomware attack ever occurred in May 2017 with the **WannaCry** attacks that infected over 200,000 Windows systems including computers at 48 hospital trusts in the United Kingdom, crippling operations. The attack spread to European countries and to the U.S., and even included attacks that compromised medical devices.[11]

Hackers know that daily hospital operations depend on IT systems and that often management will decide to pay rather than disrupt operations. In early 2017, Hollywood Presbyterian declared an internal emergency and paid $17,000 to rogue hackers to unlock their files. The hospital was able to resume normal operations. But another hospital took the opposite approach. Erie County Medical Center (ECMC) in Buffalo, New York, was hit with a ransomware attack—but management decided not to pay the $30,000 ransom, and to go to manual operations until every computer could be scanned, cleaned, and restored.[12] The disruption lasted over six weeks and cost ECMC nearly $10 million.

Hackers are getting more sophisticated and savvy. They recently introduced **Ransomware-as-a-Service** kits that they sell to other rogue operators, which can be customized to hit a particular target. Often the developer of the kit will take a percentage of the proceeds of successful ransomware attacks.[13]

Compliance and Legal Risks

There are additional compliance and legal risks to identify and research. Federal, provincial, state, and even municipal laws and regulations may apply to the retention period for business or patient information. Organizations operating in multiple jurisdictions must maintain compliance with laws and regulations that may cross national, state, or provincial boundaries. Legally required privacy requirements and retention periods must be researched for each jurisdiction (state, country) in which the business operates, so that it complies with all applicable laws.

Legal counsel and records managers (or the IG Lead) must conduct their own legislative research to apprise themselves of mandatory information retention requirements, as well as privacy considerations and requirements, especially in regard to PHI and PII. This information must be analyzed and structured and then presented to legal staff for discussion. Then further legal and regulatory research must be conducted, and firm legal opinions must be rendered by the organization's legal counsel regarding information retention, and privacy and security requirements in accordance with laws and regulations. This is an absolute requirement. The legal staff or outside legal counsel should provide input as to the **Legal Hold Notification** (LHN) process, provide opinions and interpretations of law that applies to a particular organization, and provide input on the value of formal records to arrive at a consensus on records that have legal value to the organization, and to construct an appropriate retention schedule.

Legal requirements trump all others. The retention period for PHI data or a particular type of record series must meet minimum retention, privacy, and security requirements as mandated by law. Business needs and other considerations are secondary. So, legal research is required before determining and implementing retention periods, privacy policies, and security measures. In identifying information requirements and risks, legal requirements trump all others.

In order to locate the regulations and citations relating to retention of records, there are two basic approaches. The first approach is to use a Records Retention Citation Service, which publishes in electronic form all of the retention-related citations. These services are usually purchased on a subscription basis, as the citations are updated on an annual or more frequent basis as legislation and regulations change.

Another approach is to search the laws and regulations directly, using online or print resources. Records retention requirements for corporations operating in the United States may be found in the **Code of Federal Regulations** (CFR). "The Code of Federal Regulations (CFR) annual edition is the codification of the general and permanent rules published in the Federal Register by the departments and agencies of the federal government. It is divided into 50 titles that represent broad areas subject to federal regulation."[14]

For governmental agencies, a key consideration is complying with requests for information as a result of the U.S. Freedom of Information Act (FOIA), Freedom of Information Act 2000 (in the U.K.), and similar legislation in other countries. So the process of governing information is critical to meeting these requests by the public for governmental records.

Step 2: Determine the Potential Financial and Operational Impact of the Identified Adverse Events

Benchmarking data from peer organizations provides reasonable projections of potential financial and operational impact. A list of major breaches and ransomware attacks and their costs should be considered in the calculations of financial impact. Also, a list of major HIPAA non-compliance fines at peer organizations provides a baseline for estimating the potential cost of violations. These estimates should then be normalized and brought into line with the size of an organization, with considerations given to the competitive, regulatory, and economic environment within which it operates.

Step 3: Weigh the Likelihood that the Identified Risk Events will Materialize

In this step, percentages are assigned to the potential adverse events that have been identified. Whereas a major breach event could cost the organization, say, $5 million dollars, its likelihood may be low, in the 3%–5% range. Risk management professionals may use certain methodologies to assess the likelihood that an event may occur. Or senior management may have internal models developed to assess risk likelihood. Absent standard methodologies, the IG steering committee should utilize their experience and information from external input to assess the likelihood that an adverse event may occur.

Once percentages have been assigned, an "**expected value**" (EV) calculation can be made. For instance, if a major breach would cost $5 million dollars, and its likelihood is 5%, then the expected value of the financial impact of that event for planning and risk-ranking purposes is:

$$EV = \$5,000,000 \times 5\% = \$250,000$$

If the exposure from a HIPAA violation has led to fines in the $2 million range, but the organization holds a fairly weak compliance posture, perhaps the likelihood is 10%. The EV calculation would then be:

$$EV = \$2,000,000 \times 10\% = \$200,000$$

And in like manner the potential financial impact of other identified risk events may be calculated, so they can then be ranked and prioritized. This gives executive management the information they need to make budget decisions. Certainly, the risks that are most likely to have a greater financial impact are those that must be mitigated as a priority.

Many organizations create a formalized **risk profile** to more accurately assess risks the organization faces.

Creating a risk profile is a basic building block in **enterprise risk management** (yet *another* "ERM"), which assists executives in understanding the risks associated with stated business objectives, and allocating resources, within a structured evaluation approach or framework. There are multiple ways to create a risk profile, and how often it is done, the external sources consulted, and stakeholders who have input will vary from organization to organization.[15] A key tenet to bear in mind is that *simpler is better*, and that sophisticated tools and techniques should not make the process overly complex.

According to ISO, risk is defined as "the effect of uncertainty on objectives" and a **risk profile** is "a description of a set of risks."[16] Creating a risk profile involves identifying, documenting, assessing, and prioritizing risks that an organization may face in pursuing its business objectives. Those associated risks can be evaluated and delineated within a risk or IG framework.

The corporate risk profile should be an informative tool for executive management, the CEO, and the board of directors, so it should reflect that tone. In other words, it should be clear, succinct, and simplified. A risk profile may also serve to inform the head of a division or subsidiary, in which case it may contain more detail. The process can also be applied to public and nonprofit entities.

The time horizon for a risk profile varies but looking out three to five years is a good rule of thumb.[17] The risk profile typically will be created annually, although semi-annually would serve the organization better and account for changes in the business, legal, and technology environment. But if an organization is competing in a market sector with rapid business cycles or volatility, the risk profile should be generated more frequently, perhaps quarterly.

There are different types of risk profile methodologies, with a "**Top Ten**" list, **risk map**, and **heat map** being commonly used. The first is a simple identification and ranking of the 10 greatest risks in relation to business objectives. The risk map is a visual tool that is easy to grasp, with a grid depicting a likelihood axis and an impact axis, usually rated on a scale of 1–5. In a risk assessment meeting, stakeholders can weigh in on risks using voting technology to generate a consensus. A heat map is a color-coded matrix generated by stakeholders voting on risk level by color (e.g. red being highest).

Information gathering is a fundamental activity in building the risk profile. Surveys are good for gathering basic information, but for more detail, a good method to employ is direct, person-to-person interviews, beginning with executives and risk professionals.[18] Select a representative cross-section of functional groups to gain a broad view. Depending on the size of the organization, you may need to conduct 20–40 interviews, with one person asking the questions and probing, while another team member takes notes and asks occasionally for clarification or elaboration. Conduct the interviews in a compressed timeframe—knock them out within one to three weeks and do not drag the process out, as business conditions and personnel can change over the course of months.

There are a number of helpful considerations to conducting successful interviews. First, prepare some questions for the interviewee in advance, so they may prepare and do some of their own research. Secondly, schedule the interview close to their office, and at their convenience. Thirdly, keep the time as short as possible, but long enough to get the answers you will need; approximately 20–45 minutes. Be sure to leave some open time between interviews to collect your thoughts and prepare for the next one. And follow up with interviewees after analyzing and distilling the notes to confirm that you have gained the correct insights.

The information the IG team will be harvesting will vary depending on the interviewee's level and function. You will need to look for any hard data or reports that show performance and trends related to information risk. There may be benchmarking data available as well. Delve into information access and security policies, policy development, policy adherence, and the like. Ask questions about the EHR and ePHI and privacy risks. Ask about retention of e-mail and legal hold processes. Ask about records retention and disposition policies. Ask about long-term preservation of digital records. Ask about their data deletion policies. Ask for documentation regarding IG-related training and communications. Dig into policies for access to confidential data and vital records. Try to get a real sense of the way things are run, what is standard operating procedure, and also how workers might get around overly restrictive policies, or operate without clear policies. Learn enough so that you can grasp the management style and corporate culture, and then distill that information into your findings.

Key events and developments must also be included in the risk profile. For instance, loss or potential loss of a major lawsuit, or pending regulatory changes that could impact your IG policies, or a change in business ownership or structure must all be accounted for and factored into the information risk profile. Even changes in governmental leadership should be considered, if they might impact IG policies. These types of developments should be tracked on a regular basis, and should continue to feed into the risk equation.[19] You must observe and incorporate an analysis of key events in developing and updating the risk profile.

At this point, it should be possible to generate a list of specific potential risks. It may be useful to group or categorize the potential risks into clusters such as natural disaster, regulatory, safety, competitive, technological and so forth. Armed with this list of risks, you should solicit input from stakeholders as to likelihood and timing of the threats or risks. As the organization matures in its risk identification and handling capabilities, a good practice is to look at the risks and their ratings from the previous years to attempt to gain insights into change and trends—both external and internal—that affected the risks.

Step 4: Create High-Level Strategic Plans to Mitigate the Greatest Risks

After identifying the major risk events the organization faces and calculating the potential financial impact, the IG Steering Committee must develop possible countermeasures to reduce the risks, and their impact if they do occur. This means creating an **information risk mitigation plan**. Various risk mitigation options should be explored for each major risk, and then the required tasks to reduce the specified risks and improve the odds of achieving business objectives should be delineated.[20] Considering all the documentation that has been collected and analyzed in creating the risk profile and risk assessment, the specific tasks and accountabilities should be laid out and documented. The information risk mitigation plan must include key milestones and metrics and a timetable for implementation of the recommended risk mitigation measures. Some of the major tasks will include developing a robust and consistent security awareness training program, acquiring new IT tools, developing risk countermeasure implementation plans, and assigning roles and responsibilities to carry them out.

A helpful exercise and visual tool is to draw up a table of top risks, their potential impact, and actions that have been taken to mitigate the risk.

Step 5: Develop Strategic Plans into Specific Policies

The strategic plans will be high level and must be forged into everyday policies to embed IG considerations into daily operations. Creating or updating policies in multiple areas will be required, along with metrics to measure how well the information risk mitigation is being implemented. Some policy areas that may need to be reviewed include: overall privacy policy; e-mail policies, specifically when handling PHI (or PII or PCI); text messaging policies when handling PHI; instant messaging policies when handling PHI; social media use policies; mobile device policies, especially when handling PHI; policies for the use of cloud computing platforms; if the organization uses SharePoint, there must be updated governance policies on the appropriate use of the portal; personnel policies, especially when handling PHI, and other areas as needed by a specific organization.

Step 6: Determine Metrics to Measure Risk Reductions from Mitigation Efforts

The IG program must be measured and controlled. Objective ways to measure conformance and performance of the program must be developed. This requires quantitative measures that are meaningful and measure progress. Stakeholder consultation is required in order that meaningful metrics are created.

Determining relevant ways of measuring progress will allow executives to see progress, as, realistically, *reducing risk is not something anyone can see or feel*—it is only in the failure to do so, when the risk comes home to roost, when the painful realizations are made. Also, valid metrics help to justify investment in the IG program.

The proper metrics and milestones will vary from organization to organization. Below are some examples of specific metrics:

- Reduce the number of medical errors due to poor or untimely information by 10% over the previous fiscal year.
- Reduce the data lost on stolen or misplaced laptops by 50% over the previous fiscal year.
- Reduce the number of hacker intrusion events that penetrate the perimeter by 25% over the previous fiscal year.
- Reduce e-discovery costs by 25% for document review (per GB) over the previous fiscal year.
- Reduce the number of adverse findings in the risk and compliance audit by 25% over the previous fiscal year.
- Roll out the implementation of encryption software to protect sensitive information to 50 users this fiscal year.
- Provide confidential messaging services for the organization's 10 top executives this fiscal year.

An organization's IG program metrics should be tailored and should tie directly to stated business objectives.

Step 7: Identify Those Who Are Accountable for Executing the New Risk Mitigating Processes and Maintaining the Processes in Place

From the IG steering committee, specific individuals should be assigned to be held accountable for specific tasks that are set out in the information risk mitigation plan. Sometimes this may mean a small team, a sub-group of the larger IG steering committee, is assigned accountability, since IG crosses functional boundaries. Generally, those individuals who have expertise in a certain area are best to assign accountabilities in their area. For instance, if the organization is planning to encrypt all PHI when transmitted, the HIM manager and IT manager (or IT representative) will need to work together to roll out the new capability, and to develop a training and communications plan.

Step 8: Execute the Risk Mitigation Plan

Executing the risk mitigation plan requires that regular project team meetings are set up, and key reports on the information risk mitigation metrics are developed to manage the process.

Standard project/program management tools and techniques should be utilized, as they are proven. Some additional tools may be needed, such as leveraging collaboration software, knowledge management software, or even social media within the organization.

The most important part of managing an IG program is clear and regular communications, to keep the team updated and motivated, and to smoke out any rising problems or challenges. Everyone on the IG team must be kept up to date on the progress being made in the information risk reduction effort.

Step 9: Audit the Information Risk Mitigation Plan

It may be wise to use an internal auditor, or even an external auditor or consultant to measure the progress of the information risk mitigation plan, based on the metrics established by the IG team. The output of the audit process will provide useful input for fine-tuning and improving the program. The output should not be viewed so much as a punitive tool, but one to continually improve the program over time.

What are the Risks?	How Might They Impact Business Objectives?	Actions and Processes Currently in Place?	Additional Resources Needed to Manage this Risk?	Action by Whom?	Action by When?	Done
Breach of confidential documents	Compromise confidential information Compromise competitive position Compromise business negotiations	Utilizing ITIL and CobiT IT frameworks Published security policies Semi-annual security audits	Implement newer technologies including Information Rights Management (IRM) Implement quarterly audits	IT staff, security officer	01/10/2020	01/10/2020

To summarize, a risk assessment can be compressed into five basic steps:[21]

1. **Identify the risks**. This should be an output of creating a risk profile, but if conducting a risk assessment, first identify the major information-related risks.
2. **Determine potential impact**. If a calculation of a range of economic impact is possible (e.g. lose $10 M in legal damages), then include it. If not, be as specific as possible as to how a negative event related to an identified risk can impact business objectives.
3. **Evaluate risk levels and probabilities and recommend action**. This may be in the form of recommending new procedures or processes, new investments in information technology, or other actions to mitigate identified risks.
4. **Create a report with recommendations and implement**. This may include a risk assessment table as well as written recommendations; then implement.
5. **Review periodically**. Audit annually or semi-annually, as appropriate for your organization.

Chapter Summary: Key Points

- **Information risk planning is an essential activity in IG programs**
- Healthcare organizations face major risks from data breaches, ransomware attacks, HIPAA compliance, and other legal risks.
- In identifying information requirements and risks, legal requirements trump all others.
- The risk profile is a high-level, executive decision input tool which helps to gauge risks.
- A common risk profile method is to create a prioritized or ranked "Top Ten" list of greatest risks to information.
- Once a list of risks is developed, grouping them into basic categories (e.g. natural disaster, technology, compliance) helps stakeholders better understand them.
- The risk mitigation plan develops risk reduction options and tasks to reduce specified risks.
- Expected value is a calculation to determine the relative financial impact of a specified risk.
- Metrics are required to measure progress in the risk mitigation plan.
- Audits provide feedback on the progress of the risk mitigation plan.

Notes

1. Elizabeth Snell, "The Role of Risk Assessments in Healthcare," *Health IT Security*, https://healthitsecurity.com/features/the-role-of-risk-assessments-in-healthcare.
2. "Summary of the HIPAA Security Rule," Office for Civil Rights (OCR), last reviewed July 26, 2013, https://www.hhs.gov/hipaa/for-professionals/security/laws-regulations/index.html.
3. Eric Basu, "Implementing A Risk Management Framework For Health Information Technology Systems-NIST RMF," Forbes.com, August 3, 2013, http://www.forbes.com/sites/ericbasu/2013/08/03/implementing-a-risk-management-framework-for-health-information-technology-systems-nist-rmf/#23e63d46523a.
4. Ryan Francis, "Ransomware Makes Healthcare Wannacry," CSOOnline, May 15, 2017, https://www.csoonline.com/article/3196827/data-breach/ransomware-makes-healthcare-wannacry.html.
5. "HIPAA Fines Listed by Year," Compliancy Group, https://compliancy-group.com/hipaa-fines-directory-year.
6. Sarah Kuranda, "The 10 Biggest Data Breaches Of 2016 (So Far)," CRN.com, July 28, 2016, http://www.crn.com/slide-shows/security/300081491/the-10-biggest-data-breaches-of-2016-so-far.htm/pgno/0/1.
7. "HIPAA Fines Listed by Year," Compliancy Group, https://compliancy-group.com/hipaa-fines-directory-year.
8. Ibid.
9. Ibid.
10. Jessica Davis, "Ransomware Accounted for 72% of Healthcare Malware Attacks in 2016," *Healthcare IT News*, April 27, 2017, http://www.healthcareitnews.com/news/ransomware-accounted-72-healthcare-malware-attacks-2016.
11. Thomas Fox-Brewster, "Medical Devices Hit by Ransomware for the First Time in US Hospitals," Forbes.com, May 17, 2017, https://www.forbes.com/sites/thomasbrewster/2017/05/17/wannacry-ransomware-hit-real-medical-devices/#3956264c425c.
12. Jonathan Crowe, "How One Ransomware Attack Cost Erie County Medical Center $10 Million," Barkly.com, August 2017, https://blog.barkly.com/10-million-dollar-ecmc-hospital-ransomware-attack.
13. Ibid.
14. "Code of Federal Regulations," U.S. Government Publishing Office (GPO), www.gpo.gov/help/index.html#about_code_of_federal_regulations.htm.

15. John Fraser and Betty Simkins (eds.), *Enterprise Risk Management: Today's Leading Research and Best Practices for Tomorrow's Executives* (Wiley, 2010), p. 171.
16. "ISO 31000 2009 Plain English, Risk Management Dictionary," Praxiom.com, February 4, 2017, http://www.praxiom.com/iso-31000-terms.htm.
17. John Fraser and Betty Simkins (eds.), *Enterprise Risk Management: Today's Leading Research and Best Practices for Tomorrow's Executives* (Wiley, 2010), p. 172.
18. Ibid.
19. Ibid. p. 179.
20. A Guide to the Project Management Body of Knowledge (PMBOK Guide), 4th ed. (Project Management Institute, 2008), pp. 273–312.
21. "Controlling the Risks in the Workplace," Health and Safety Executive, http://www.hse.gov.uk/risk/controlling-risks.htm.

Chapter 9

Strategic Planning and Best Practices for IG

Start with Business Objectives

The IG team should begin their strategic planning process by listing and prioritizing key organizational objectives. These objectives may be quite broad; keep the list short. Then, put questions up for discussion such as:

"What discrete projects can we form and execute to contribute to the accomplishment of our overall business objectives?"

"What information do we need to help complete and maintain these projects?"

"How long will the information have business value?"

"How can we leverage the business value of this information?"

and so forth.

Align the IG Plan with Strategic Plans

The IG plan must support the achievement of the organization's business objectives, and therefore should be melded into the overall strategic plan for the organization. Integration with the strategic plan means that pursuing the business objectives in the IG plan are consistent with, and in support of, the enterprise strategic plan.

So, for example, if a particular medical center has been hit with some major lawsuits due to medical mistakes, then a program emphasizing data governance and data quality would directly address medical error issues. Perhaps a new Chief Data Officer position is created, and perhaps new software is needed for data cleansing and scrubbing to reduce the incidence of inaccurate data.

Or if the corporate strategy includes plans for acquiring smaller competitors and folding them into the organization's structure as operating divisions, then the IG plan must assist and contribute to this effort. Plans for standardizing operating policies and procedures among the new acquisitions must include a consistent, systematized approach to key principles of IG, including stakeholder consultation, user training and communications, and compliance audits.

The IG plan should bring a standard approach across the spectrum of information use and management within the organization and must be forged to accommodate the new acquisitions. This means that patient ID verification policies, privacy notices and policies, litigation readiness policies—even general office policies for e-mail, mobile device use, social media use, cloud collaboration, and storage use—must be consistent and aligned with the overall strategic plan. *In other words, the goal is to get all employees on the "same page" and working to support the business objectives of the strategic plan in everyday small steps within the IG plan.*

The organization will also have an IT strategic plan, which must be aligned with the organizational strategic plan to support overall business objectives. The IT strategy may be to convert new acquisitions to the internal financial and accounting systems of the organization, and to train newly-acquired employees to use the existing software applications under the umbrella of the IG plan. Or the IT plan may be to move to cloud computing, so cloud-based solutions should be focused upon primarily. Again, the IG plan needs to be integrated with the IT strategy and must consider the organization's approach to IT.

The result of the process of aligning the IG effort with the IT strategy and the organization's overall strategic plan will mean, ideally, that employee efforts are more efficient and productive since they are consistently moving toward the achievement of the organization's overall strategic goals. The organization will be healthier, and will have less dissent and confusion, with clear IG policies that leverage the IT strategy and help pursue overall business objectives.

There are further considerations that must be folded into the IG plan. As every corporate culture is different, and has a real impact on decision-making and operational approaches, it must be considered. Corporate culture includes the organization's appetite for risk, its use of IT (e.g. forward thinking "first adopter"), its capital investment strategies, and other management actions.

If, say, the organization is conservative and risk averse, it may want to hold off on implementing some emerging e-discovery technologies that can cut costs but also introduce greater risk. Or, if it is an aggressive, progressive, risk-taking organization, it may opt to test and adopt newer e-discovery technologies, under the IT strategy and the umbrella of IG policies. An example may be the use of predictive coding technology in early case assessment (ECA). Predictive coding uses text auto-classification technology and neural technology with the assistance of human input to "learn" which e-documents might be responsive in a particular legal matter, and which may not be. Through a series of steps of testing and checking subsets of the documents, human experts provide input to improve the sorting and selection process. The software uses machine learning (artificial intelligence whereby the software can change and improve on a particular task, as its decision engine is shaped and "trained" by input) to improve its ability to cull through and sort documents.

Predictive coding can reduce e-discovery costs, yet there are risks that the approach can be challenged in court and could, in fact, affect the case adversely. So it is clear to see how a decision on a technology like predictive coding can involve and include elements of the IG plan, IT strategy, and overall organizational strategic plan.

And there are resource issues to consider: How much management time or "bandwidth" is available to pursue the IG plan development and execution? Is there a budget item to allow for software acquisitions and training and communications to support the execution of the IG plan? Obviously, without the allocated management time and budget money, the IG plan cannot be executed.

Survey and Evaluate External Factors

The IG plan is now harmonized and aligned with the organization's strategic plan and IT strategy, but you are not finished yet, because it cannot survive in a vacuum; organizations must analyze and consider the external business, legal, and technological environment and fold their analysis into their plans.

Analyze Information Technology Trends

IG requires IT to support and monitor implementation of polices, so it matters what is developing and trending in the information technology space. What new technologies are coming online? Is the organization tracking the use of blockchain, artificial intelligence (AI), and the Internet of Things (IoT) in healthcare? Why are they being developed and becoming popular? How do these changes in the business environment that created opportunities for new technologies to be developed affect the organization and its ability to execute its IG plan? How can new technologies assist? Which ones are immature and too risky? These are some of the questions that must be addressed in regard to the changing information technology landscape.

Some changes in information and communications technology (ICT) are rather obvious, such as the trends toward mobile computing, tablet and smartphone devices, cloud storage, and social media use. Each one of these major trends that may affect or assist in implementing IG needs to be considered, and again, this must be done within the framework of the organization's strategic plan and IT strategy. If the corporate culture is progressive and supportive of remote work and telecommuting, and the organizational strategy aims to lower fixed costs by reducing the amount of fixed office space for employees and moving to a more mobile workforce, then trends in tablet and smartphone computing that are relevant to the organization must be analyzed and considered. Is the organization going to provide mobile devices, or support a bring-your-own-device (BYOD) environment? Which equipment and technologies will be supported? iOS, Android, or both? What is the policy going to be on phone jacking/modification? What is the IG policy regarding confidential documents on mobile devices? Will the organization use encryption extensively? If so, which software? Is the enterprise moving to the cloud computing model? Utilizing social media? What about Big Data? Is the organization going to consider deploying auto-classification and predictive coding technologies? What are the trends that might affect the organization?

There are many, many questions that must be addressed, but the evaluation must be narrowed down to those technology trends that specifically might impact the execution of the IG plan, and rollout of new technology.

On a more granular level, evaluate even supported file and document formats. It gets that detailed, when crafting IG policy. For instance, PDF/A is the standard format for archiving electronic documents. So plans must include long-term digital preservation (LTDP) standards and Best Practices.

Survey Business Conditions and Economic Environment

If the economy is on a down cycle, and particularly if the healthcare business sector has been negatively affected, resources may be scarcer than in better times, and hence, it may be more difficult to get budget approval for necessary program expenses, such as new technologies, staff, contractors, training materials, and so forth. This means the IG plan may need to be scaled back, or its scope reduced. Implementing the plan in a key division rather than attempting an enterprise rollout is the best tactic in tough economic times, and at all times, actually. Start small.

But if things are booming, and the business is growing fast, then budget money for investments in the IG program may be easier to secure, and the goals may be expanded.

IG should be an ongoing program, but it takes time to implement, and it takes resources to execute, audit, and continue to refine. So an executive looking for a quick and calculable payback on the investment may want to focus on narrower areas. For instance, the focus may be entirely on security awareness training, or the legal hold and e-discovery process initially, with business objectives that include reducing pre-trial costs and attorney fees by a certain percentage or amount. It is much easier to see concrete results when focusing on e-discovery, since legal costs are real, and will always be there. However, if the IG effort is broader and improves the ability to organize and search for information faster, and to execute more complete searches to improve the basis for management decision-making, the business case may be more difficult to make. Improved management decision-making will improve the organization's competitiveness long term, but it may be difficult to cite specific examples where costs were saved or revenues were increased as a result of the "better decisions" that should come about through better information governance.

Analyze Relevant Legal, Regulatory, and Political Factors

In consultation with the legal team or lead, the laws and regulations that affect the organization's segment in the healthcare industry should be identified. Narrowing the scope of the analysis, those that specifically could impact the governance of information should be considered and analyzed. What absolute requirements do they impose? Where there is room for interpretation, where, legally, does the organization want to position itself? How much legal risk is acceptable? These are the types of questions that legal and risk management professionals can assist in making. Again, legal requirements trump all others.

The decision process must include considerations for the future and anticipated future changes. Changes in the legal and regulatory environment happen based on the political leaders who are in place, and any pending legislation. Therefore, go further and analyze the current political environment, and make some judgments based on the best information, the organization's culture and appetite for risk, management style, available resources, and other factors. Generally, a more conservative environment means less regulation, and this analysis must also be folded into the IG strategic plan.

Survey and Determine Industry Best Practices

Information governance is a developing hybrid "super discipline" that is a superset of data governance cyber-security, information privacy, HIM and records management, e-discovery, analytics, and more. IG emerged to help manage the explosion in the amount of information that must be managed in today's increasingly regulated and litigious business environment. As such, Best Practices are still being formed and expanded. This process of testing, proving, and sharing Best Practices will continue for the next decade as Best Practices are expanded, revised, and refined.

The most relevant study of IG Best Practices is one that is conducted for the organization which surveys the organization's segment of the healthcare industry and even what some of its more progressive competitors are doing in regard to IG. Often, engaging a third-party consultant is the best way to get this accomplished, since they can more easily contact, interview, and research competitors' practices. But also, there is assistance available from trade associations such as HIMSS, AHIMA, and others which can provide some consensus as to emerging Best Practices in healthcare IG.

Below is a sampling of broad IG Best Practices that will help guide the program. These are a starting point; you must conduct research and uncover Best Practices specific to the goals of the IG program to make them meaningful guidelines to drive the IG effort:

1. **Executive sponsorship is crucial.** Securing an executive sponsor at the senior management level is key to successful IG programs. It is not possible to require managers to take time out of their other duties to participate in a project if there is no executive edict. The executive sponsor must *own* the business case for the IG program and have a long-term vested interest in its success. It is advisable to also have a deputy executive sponsor to help support the program and assure the durability of IG program leadership.

2. **Establish a cross-functional IG council or steering committee.** There must be a holistic view of information use in the organization, which seeks to leverage it as an asset and to reduce its risks and costs. At a minimum, there must be representation from Legal, HIM, IT, Privacy, Information Security, Finance, and Human Resources, and depending on the organization and its focus, perhaps other key groups such as Risk Management, Data Governance, Analytics, Knowledge Management, and more.

3. **Create a formal IG Program Charter for guidance.** It should include the overall mission and goals of the IG program and should list IG committee members and their basic responsibilities, as well as the meeting schedule. It also should show the reporting structure of the IG committee members and delineate their basic program responsibilities. It is advisable to form a small, top-tier "decision committee" to facilitate decisions and recommendations made to the executive sponsor. The IG Program Charter should be signed off on by the executive sponsor.

4. **Develop an overall organizational strategy for the IG program.** This will ensure there is agreement on the aims and foci of the program and help the various functional groups involved to collaborate and cooperate to execute the IG program strategy. "An over-arching strategy is needed—including patient care, organizational performance and risk mitigation—to establish organization's goals and priorities, and consistently drive these through information systems and business processes."[1]

5. **IG is not a project but, rather, an ongoing program.** IG programs are "evergreen" and should eventually become embedded into routine operations. True, there must be discrete projects executed under the overall IG program, which provides an umbrella of guidelines and policies. Performance is monitored and enforced with the support of metrics, information technologies, and audit tools.

   Compare the IG program to a workplace safety program which is continuously improved, reinforced, and expanded; every time a new location, team member, piece of equipment, or toxic substance is acquired by the organization, the workplace safety program dictates how that is handled and, if it doesn't, workplace safety policies/procedures/training need to be updated. The program must be monitored and audited to ensure the program is followed and to make adjustments. The effort never ends.[2]

6. **Using an IG framework or maturity model is helpful in assessing and guiding IG programs.** Various models are offered, perhaps the most comprehensive being the **Information Governance Process Maturity Model** (IGPMM) from the Compliance, Governance, and Oversight Council (CGOC), released in 2012 and updated and expanded in 2017 to include privacy and data protection obligations, GDPR considerations, a new data security cost lever, cloud computing safeguards, a greater focus on data governance, and other considerations. The IGPMM rates IG programs in detail on 22 processes, with a heavy emphasis

on Legal, Privacy, and Security.[3] Other models include AHIMA's IG Adaption Model and *IGHealthRate*™, which developed the health sector use; and the Generally Accepted Recordkeeping Principles® ("The Principles") Maturity Model from ARMA International, which is most appropriately used to evaluate the maturity of general recordkeeping (e.g. in the Business Office).

7. **Business processes must be redesigned when implementing electronic health records (EHR) to streamline operations and improve the accuracy and management of electronic protected health information (ePHI)**. Using EHR fundamentally changes the way people work and greater efficiencies and control can be gained with business process redesign (versus simply using EHR systems as a rote electronic filing cabinet).

8. **Leverage analytics to improve clinical decision support planning, decision-making, and outcomes**. The entire range of analytics, from descriptive to predictive to prescriptive analytics, must be deployed to fully exploit data value.[4] It is crucial to have a robust data governance program in place to assure data quality so the analytics are accurate. Beyond that, the organization should look for ways to monetize data, either directly or indirectly.

9. **Focus data governance efforts heavily on data quality**. Improved data quality and availability will help reduce medical errors, improve patient satisfaction, improve population health, and improve financial performance.

10. **Creating standardized metadata terms should be part of an IG effort that enables faster, more complete, and more accurate searches and retrieval of records**. This is important not only in everyday clinical operations, but also in business operations. Good metadata management also assists in the maintenance of corporate memory and improving accountability in business operations.[5] Using a standardized format and controlled vocabulary provides a "precise and comprehensible description of content, location, and value."[6] Using a controlled vocabulary means the organization has standardized a set of terms used for metadata elements describing records. This ensures consistency and helps with optimizing search and retrieval functions, as well as meeting e-discovery requests, compliance demands, and other legal and regulatory requirements.

Formulating the IG Strategic Plan

Now comes the time to make sense of all the information and input the IG team has gathered and hammer it into a workable IG strategic plan. This will involve some give-and-take among IG team members, each having their own perspective and priorities. Everyone will be lobbying for their functional group's view, but it is the job of the executive sponsor to set the tone. They must emphasize organizational business objectives so that the effort does not drag out or turn into a competition but, rather, a well-informed consensus development process that results in a clear, workable IG strategic plan.

Synthesize Gathered Information and Fuse into IG Strategy

The IG team has gathered a great deal of information that needs to be analyzed and distilled into actionable strategies. This process will depend on the expertise and specialized knowledge the IG team brings to the table within the construct of the organizational culture. The IG team must be able to make decisions and establish priorities that bear in mind organizational business objectives and consider a number of influencing factors.

Do not prolong the strategy development process; the longer it becomes, the more key factors influencing it can change.

Aim to develop a strategic plan that is durable enough to withstand changes in the business environment, technology, legislation, and other key influencing factors, but it should be relevant to that snapshot of information that was collected early on. When all the parts and pieces start changing, and require reconsideration, it does not serve the organization well. Focus is needed.

Develop high-level IG strategies for each of the critical areas, including data governance/ePHI quality, information security awareness training, patient privacy, the legal hold process, e-discovery action plans, e-mail policy, mobile computing policy, vital records and disaster planning, and other areas that are important to the organization. Do this first, without regard to the prioritization of these areas, to maintain focus.

Then go through the hard process of prioritizing strategies and aligning them to organizational goal and objectives. This may not be difficult in the beginning. For instance, IG strategies for improving clinical data quality are going to take higher priority than the social media policy, and protecting vital records is paramount to any organization. Yet, as the process progresses it will become more challenging to make tradeoffs and establish priorities. Then tie these strategies to overall organizational goals and business objectives.

A good technique to keep goals and objectives in mind may be to post them prominently in the meeting room where these strategy sessions take place. This will help to keep the IG team focused.

Develop Actionable Plans to Support Organizational Goals and Objectives

Plans and policies to support IG efforts must be developed that identify specific tasks and steps, and define roles and responsibilities for those who will be held accountable for their implementation. Execution is critical, although the team cannot simply create the plan and marching orders: periodic checks and audits must be built in to test that new IG policies are being followed, and that they have hit their mark. Invariably, there will be adjustments, and the adjustments must be continually made to craft the policies for maximum effectiveness and continued relevance in the face of changes in external factors, such as legislation and business competition, and internal changes in management style and structure.

Create New IG Driving Programs to Support Business Goals and Objectives

The IG program needs a spark to ignite action and signal change to employees. If employees do not see changes, understand the "why" of the effort, and how it contributes to overall organizational objectives, they will lack motivation. Launching new sub-programs within the overall IG program is a good way to start. For instance, a new information security awareness training (SAT) initiative can show almost immediate results, as it reduces information risk immediately and on an ongoing basis. Another initiative may focus on ePHI data quality, with the goal of reducing medical errors and improving patient satisfaction. Or the organization may want to revamp the **legal hold notification** (LHN) process to make it more complete and verifiable, assigning specific employees specific tasks to be accountable for. Part of that effort may be evaluating and implementing new technology assisted review (TAR) processes and predictive coding technology. Working cooperatively on smaller parts of the overall IG program is a way to show real results within defined timeframes. Piecing together a series of program components is the best way to get started and it breaks the overall IG program down into digestible, doable chunks. A small win early on is crucial to maintain momentum and executive sponsorship.

To be clear, the IG team will need to negotiate and agree on the success metrics the program will be measured on in advance.

Draft the IG Strategic Plan and Gain Input from a Broader Group of Stakeholders

Once the pieces of the plan are drafted and the IG team is in agreement that it has been harmonized and aligned with overall organizational goals and objectives, test the waters to see if the plan holds up with a broader audience. Expose a broader group of stakeholders to the plan to gain their input. Perhaps the IG team has become myopic, or has passed over some points that are important to the broader stakeholder audience. So solicit and discuss their input and, to the degree that there is a consensus, refine the IG strategic plan one last time before finalizing it. Bear in mind, though, that it is a living document, a work-in-progress, which will require revisiting and updating to assure it is in step with changing external and internal factors. Periodic auditing and review of the plan will reveal areas that need to be adjusted and revised to keep the plan relevant and effective.

Get Buy-In and Sign-Off and Execute the Plan

Have the executive sponsor sign-off on the IG Strategic Plan. Then present the finalized plan to executive management, preferably including the CEO, and demonstrate what is required and its intended benefits. Field questions and address any concerns to gain broader executive buy-in and perhaps more signatures. Some minor adjustments may be required if there are significant objections, but, if the stakeholder consultation process was executed properly, the plan show be very close to the mark. Then begin the process of implementing the IG strategic plan including regular status meetings and updates, consistent and regular communications and training, and planned audits of activities.

Chapter Summary: Key Points

- **The IG team should begin their strategic planning process by listing and prioritizing key organizational objectives.**
- The IG plan must support the achievement of the organization's business objectives.
- The IG plan should bring a standard approach across the spectrum of information use and management within the organization.
- The IG strategic plan must be aligned with the IT strategic plan and the organizational strategic plan to support overall business objectives.
- The most relevant IG Best Practices to consider are those from the organization's segment of the healthcare industry.
- Engaged and invested executive sponsors are necessary for IG program success. It is not possible to require managers to take time out of their other duties otherwise.
- The executive sponsor must be: (a) directly tied to the success of the program, (b) fully engaged and aware in the program, and (c) actively eliminating barriers and resolving issues.
- The information risk mitigation plan develops risk reduction options and tasks to reduce specified risks and improve the odds for achieving business objectives.
- The IG strategic plan must be informed with an assessment of relevant technology trends.

- Include trends and conditions in the internal and external business environment in IG program planning.
- Laws and regulations relevant to the organization's management and distribution of information in all jurisdictions must be considered and included in the IG strategic plan.
- Legal requirements take priority over all others.
- Fuse the findings of all the analyses of external and internal factors into the IG strategic plan. Develop strategies and then prioritize them.
- Create supporting sub-programs to jumpstart the IG program effort. Smaller programs should be able to measure real results based upon metrics that are agreed upon in advance.
- The executive sponsor must sign off on the IG strategic plan before moving to execute it.

Notes

1. "Best Practices by Industry: Healthcare," InfoGovBasics.com, https://www.infogovbasics.com/best-practices/by-industry/healthcare.
2. Monica Crocker, e-mail to author, June 21, 2012.
3. "Latest CGOC Information Governance Process Maturity Model," CGOC, https://www.cgoc.com/updated-ig-process-maturity-model-reflects-todays-data-realities-2.
4. AHIMA Staff, "Use Cases Demonstrate Information Governance Best Practices," Journal of AHIMA website, September 30, 2014, http://journal.ahima.org/2014/09/30/use-cases-demonstrate-information-governance-best-practices/.
5. Kate Cumming, "Metadata Matters," in *Managing Electronic Records*, ed. by Julie McLeod and Catherine Hare (London: Facet Publishing, 2005), p. 34.
6. "Electronic Records Management Guidelines," Minnesota State Archives, www.mnhs.org/preserve/records/electronicrecords/ermetadata.html.

Chapter 10

Overseeing the IG Program

Maintaining the Information Governance (IG) program beyond an initial project effort is key to realizing continued and long-term benefits of IG. This means that the IG program must be "evergreen" and become an everyday part of the organization's operations and communications. There is continuing work to do after an initial IG program push, shaping and prioritizing discrete projects to execute under the umbrella of the IG program. The idea is to embed IG considerations in everyday business processes so that they become routine.

Program Communications and Training

Since IG programs are *fundamentally a change management effort*, any successful IG program must contain a well-developed communications and training component. The stakeholder audience must be made aware of the new policies and practices that are to be followed, and how this new approach contributes toward the accomplishment of the organization's goals and business objectives.

The first step in the communications plan is to identify and segment stakeholder audiences, and to customize or modify the message to the degree that is necessary to be effective. Communications to the Health Information Management (HIM) team should revolve around electronic health record (EHR) data quality and patient privacy aspects; communications with the Information Technology (IT) team should have a more technical slant; and communications to the Legal team should include some legal jargon and emphasize legal issues. The more forethought put into crafting the communications strategy, the more effective it will be.

That is not to say that *all* messages must have several versions: there are some core concepts and goals that should be emphasized in communications to all employees. Core messages include:

1. Mindfulness of information risks;
2. Emphasis on valuing information as an asset;
3. Information accuracy and quality are paramount;
4. Preserving the organization's brand and reputation are essential, and stems from providing superior patient care and guarding their PHI;
5. Stakeholder audiences must be consulted and informed as part of the IG program;

6. Information security and privacy are everyone's job and all must be mindful when handling sensitive information;
7. IG programs require continuous improvement.

Training should take multiple avenues as well. Some can be classroom instruction, some online learning, and it is a good idea to create a series of training videos (which can be in the form of recorded webinars). Aim to make the training fun and engaging. The training effort must be consistent and ongoing to maintain high levels of IG effectiveness. Certainly, this means adding IG training to the onboarding process for new hires, and for employees joining or transferring to the organization.

Program Controls, Monitoring, Auditing, and Enforcement

The only way to measure the progress and success of an IG program is to develop metrics to determine progress on training efforts, the level of employee compliance, its impact on key operational areas, cost reductions, and progress made toward established business objectives.

Testing and auditing the program provides an opportunity to give feedback to employees on how well they are doing, and coach them and recommend changes they may make. But also, having objective feedback on key metrics will allow the executive sponsor to see where progress has been made, and also, where improvements need to focus.

Although the emphasis should be on continual improvement and feedback on metrics should be used to coach employees, clear penalties for policy violations must be communicated to employees so they know the seriousness of the IG program. They must keep in mind how important it is in helping the organization pursue its business goals and accomplish stated business objectives. Penalties should be up to and including dismissal for severe violations.

Similar to a workplace safety program, ongoing training and communications are important to keep employees apprised of approved processes and behaviors which support IG. Also important is regular feedback based on established metrics to see how the IG program is progressing.

This requires vigilant and consistent monitoring and auditing to ensure that IG policies and processes are effective and consistently followed and enforced. If proper controls are in place this should become a regular part of the enterprise's operations.

Monitoring and Accountability

Monitoring and accountability in the IG program demand a continuous tightening down and expansion of protections and the implementation of emerging, strategic technologies. IT developments and innovations that can foster the effort must be steadily monitored and evaluated, and those technology subsets that can assist in providing security need to be incorporated into the mix. Some examples of newer IG-enabling technologies include advanced analytics, predictive coding, file analysis, auto-classification, artificial intelligence, blockchain, and the Internet of Things (IoT). All these and more should be on the IG steering committee radar.

The IG policies themselves—for handling PHI and confidential information, e-mail, use of social media, cloud use and so forth—must be reviewed and updated periodically to accommodate changes in the business environment, laws, regulations, and technology. Program gaps and failures must be addressed and the effort should continue to improve and adapt to new types of security threats.

IG programs emphasize accountability. Maintaining an IG program requires that an individual (or small team) is accountable for continually monitoring and refining policies and training approaches. Some individual must remain responsible for an IG policy's administration and results.[1]

Perhaps the executive sponsor for the initial project becomes the chief information governance officer (CIGO) or IG "czar" of sorts; or the chief executive officer (CEO) continues ownership of the program and drives its active improvement. The organization may also decide to make the IG steering committee a permanent one, with ongoing responsibilities for monitoring, maintaining, and advancing the program.

However it takes shape, an IG program must be evergreen, dynamic, and aggressive in its execution—and in demonstrating benefits—in order to remain effective.

Staffing Continuity Plan

In today's work environment, turnover is more frequent than in the past. People spend less time in a job before moving on to take new career opportunities outside of the organization, and also change jobs and move to other positions within an organization. So it is critical to have a staffing continuity plan for the IG steering committee so that the IG program does not have gaps or interruptions. Backup and supporting designates must be named and kept current on the administration of the program. In addition to the role of executive sponsor, an organization may have a "supporting sponsor" or "deputy sponsor" so, should the need arise, the sponsorship function maintains continuity. And likewise, there should be other staffing redundancies built in to assure the smooth and continued operation of the IG program in the event of layoffs, terminations, or unplanned incidents that threaten it.

This may mean that when the formal IG program manager is unable to be there to execute their duties, an assistant or designated backup can carry out those duties.

It is also a good idea to cross-train employees within the IG team or steering committee. With this approach, the Legal team, for instance, will better understand the needs and requirements of the HIM and Records Management functions, and vice-versa. IT must better understand the Legal department's needs. HIM should better understand Legal issues, and so forth. Cross-training improves collaboration and overall organization acceptance and understanding of the IG program, while building in safeguards to ensure it keeps running.

Continuous Process Improvement

Maintaining IG program effectiveness requires implementing principles of **continuous process improvement** (CPI). CPI is a "never-ending effort to discover and eliminate the main causes of problems." It accomplishes this by using small-steps improvements, rather than implementing one huge improvement.

In Japan, the word kaizen reflects this gradual and constant process, as it is enacted throughout the organization, regardless of department, position, or level.[2] To remain effective, the program must continue using CPI methods and techniques.

Maintaining and improving the program will require monitoring tools, periodic audits, and regular meetings for discussion and approval of changes to improve the program. It will—as emphasized in this book many times—require a cross-section of team leaders from IT, Legal, Records Management, Compliance, Internal Audit, and Risk Management, and also functional business units participating actively and presenting ideas for improvements in information-handling procedures that can improve operational efficiency, while also citing possible threats and sources of information leakage.

Why Continuous Improvement Is Needed

While the specific drivers of change are always evolving, the reasons that organizations need to continuously improve their program for securing information assets are relatively constant, and include:

- **Changing technology**. New technology capabilities need to be monitored and considered with an eye to improving, streamlining, or reducing the cost of IG. The IG program needs to anticipate new types of opportunities and threats and also evaluate adding or replacing technologies to continue to improve it.
- **Changing laws and regulations**. Compliance with new or updated laws and regulations must be maintained.
- **Internal information governance requirements**. As the organization updates and improves its overall IG, the program elements that concern critical information assets must be kept aligned and synchronized.
- **Changing business plans**. As the healthcare enterprise develops new business strategies and enters new markets, it must reconsider and update its IG program. If, for instance, an organization moves from being a local entity to a regional, national, or global one, new laws and regulations will apply, such as greater privacy and data protection demands (e.g. the new European General Data Protection Regulation), as well as new information security threats. So new privacy and security strategies and policies must be formed.
- **Evolving industry Best Practices**. Best Practices change and new Best Practices arise with the introduction of each successive wave of technology, and with changes in the business environment. The program should consider and leverage new Best Practices.
- **Fixing program shortcomings**. Addressing flaws in the IG program that are discovered through monitoring, testing, and auditing; or addressing an actual breach of confidential information; or a legal sanction or fine imposed due to non-compliance are all reasons why a program must be revisited periodically and kept updated.[3]

Maintaining the IG program requires that a senior level officer of the enterprise, the executive sponsor, continues to sponsor it and pushes for enforcement, improvement, and expansion. This requires leadership, as well as consistent and clear messaging to employees. IG and the security of information assets must be on the minds of all members of the enterprise; it must be something they are aware of and think about daily. Perhaps even IG-reinforcing messages are rotated on screen savers. Employees should be reminded to be on the lookout for ways to improve IG, and they should be rewarded for contributions made which improve program effectiveness.

Gaining this level of mindshare in employees' heads will require follow-up messages in the form of personal speeches and presentations, newsletters, corporate announcements, e-mail messages, and even posters placed at strategic points (e.g., near the shared printing station advising about secure procedures). Everyone must be reminded that keeping information assets secure is everyone's job, and that to lose, misuse, or leak confidential information harms the organization over the long term and erodes its value.

Chapter Summary: Key Points

- **Maintaining and improving the IG program requires monitoring tools and regular audits to continually improve it.**
- Lines of authority, accountability, and responsibility must be clear for the IG program to succeed long term.
- IG program communications should be consistent and clear, and customized for various stakeholder groups.
- IG program testing and audits are an opportunity to improve training and compliance, not to punish employees.
- An effective IG program requires vigilant and consistent monitoring and auditing to ensure that IG policies are followed and enforced.
- Information technologies that can assist in advancing the program must be steadily monitored, evaluated, and implemented.
- IG programs need built-in staffing redundancies to ensure their continued operation in the event of employee turnover or transfer.
- Maintaining an IG program requires that an executive sponsor continues to push for enforcement, improvement, and expansion of the program to secure and control information.

Notes

1. Mark Woeppel, "Is Your Continuous Improvement Organization a Profit Center?" PEX Network, June 3, 2009, www.processexcellencenetwork.com/process-management/articles/is-your-continuous-improvement-organization-a-prof.
2. Donald Clark, "Continuous Process Improvement," Big Dog and Little Dog's Performance Juxtaposition, March 11, 2010, www.nwlink.com/~donclark/perform/process.html.
3. Randolph A. Kahn and Barclay T. Blair, *Information Nation: Seven Keys to Information Management Compliance* (AIIM International, 2004), pp. 242–243.

INSIGHTS, STRATEGIES, AND ADVICE FROM THE FIELD

Essays and Case Studies in Information Governance

The IG Problem in Healthcare

By Mansur Hasib

Healthcare now exists within a modern world of hyper-connected networks, as is the rest of the business world. In this world, digital strategy should be a key driver for modern healthcare organizations.

This imperative is evident with the increased adoption of newer digital technologies like electronic health records (EHR), telemedicine, health information exchanges (HIE), health insurance exchanges, the Internet of Things (IoT), artificial intelligence (AI), and an array of digital patient services. So clearly, healthcare executives must implement organizational strategies in step with today's digital advancements to deliver improved patient outcomes, to guard patient data, and also to deliver financial results.

Yet healthcare executives are surprisingly still making outdated decisions—usually with drastic and expensive consequences, which include massive breaches of data, threats to patient health and safety, ransomware attacks, loss of intellectual capital, and other existential threats to the organization.

This author conducted a national study of cyber-security in healthcare in the United States (Hasib, 2013), and was very surprised to find that *top executives in half of U.S. healthcare organizations were developing digital strategies with knowledge rooted in the 1980s.*

Their anachronistic thinking harkened back to a time when programmers and technology professionals worked in finance, accounting, and human resources departments in order to support the automation of accounting, finance, and payroll.

In these organizations senior IT positions were often not represented, or were under-represented. Some had employees with the CIO title, but they reported to the chief financial officer (CFO) or other comparable executive. Therefore, quite frequently, CIOs were not empowered to make the right decisions related to Information Governance (IG) and cyber-security. They served under an organizational structure which viewed IT as a cost center instead of an investment and business driver, or perhaps even a profit center (as is suggested in the book, *Infonomics,* by Doug Laney [Taylor & Francis, 2017]).

Lack of Information Security Roles

In the same study, it was also found that one-third of U.S. healthcare organizations *did not* have a chief information security officer (CISO) or equivalent, and about one-fifth had no intention of hiring one anytime soon. This is unsustainable in today's business environment with the myriad of digital threats that organizations face.

Later, upon closer examination of some major breaches in healthcare, clear lapses in IG were found.

Finance-Driven Decisions

And it was clear that finance executives were in charge of the digital strategy—essentially a strategy driven by short-term cost reduction instead of greater considerations: protection of patient records, protection of patient trust and brand equity, protection of intellectual capital, and long-term profitability.

These situations of improper IG in healthcare organizations are extremely dangerous—both for the organization *and* for the CIO for the following key reasons:

- The CFO and other executives run cyber-security and IG strategy through budget and veto authority.
- The CIO's pay is reduced—at least a full grade level lower than it should be. Had the CIO role been on par with other executives such as the CFO, higher-quality, true digital strategists could be recruited. Most experienced CIOs would not agree to report to a CFO.
- Since CIOs are often not considered members of the executive team, they cannot participate meaningfully in organizational strategy meetings.
- Since the CIO pay is at least a rank lower, the pay for the rest of the information workers, including the chief information security officer (CISO), if such an executive exists, is also lowered. Thus acquiring and retaining top talent is extremely challenging.
- IG and cyber-security principles are rarely baked in from the beginning; rather they are overlaid in a patchwork way later, if at all, resulting in a wide range of problems.
- The CIO or CISO become ideal whipping posts for any failures; other executives are shielded, even though they make the final decisions.
- IT is not generally viewed as mission-critical and is typically outsourced because finance executives feel unqualified to lead them, and look only at expenses. This results in reduced innovation, reduced support and training of users, and depletion of internal technical talent. (Outsourcers provide exactly what is written into the contract. Innovation is not typically written into an outsourcing contract. Innovation is typically an upsell opportunity for the service providers.)
- Instead of due diligence and proper mitigation, information risks are usually transferred to third parties through insurance or other financial vehicles—usually with inadequate coverage. The inadequate coverage is typically discovered after the damage is done.

The organization chart in healthcare organizations can become the biggest cyber-security threat for the organization—a lack of proper staffing and training. This IG-related challenge must be tackled first. Also, healthcare auditors should review and address these issues in their findings. Only then can healthcare organizations begin to embark on a successful IG strategy.

Are Health Information Exchanges Properly Safeguarding ePHI? A Case Study

By Baird W. Brueseke

A regional health information exchange (HIE) contracted with information security experts to perform a security assessment of the HIE's physical office, network infrastructure, operational processes and cloud portal. This case study describes the methods used and tasks performed during the security assessment, presents lessons learned and then makes recommendations for Best Practices which should apply to all regional HIE security assessments.

Background

The governance of protected healthcare information (PHI) was originally addressed by the Heath Information Portability and Accountability Act (HIPAA), which was enacted in 1996 during the Clinton Administration. In today's interconnected world, most all PHI is electronic (ePHI).

The task of properly managing ePHI was made more complex by the Health Information Technology for Economic and Clinical Health (HITECH) Act. The HITECH Act is part of the American Recovery and Reinvestment Act (ARRA), a federal program which includes incentives for healthcare service providers to accelerate the adoption of electronic health record (EHR) systems.

Beginning in 2009, the HITECH Act authorized incentives totaling $36 billion in meaningful use funds for healthcare service providers and community grants for the formation of regional centers that foster the exchange of electronic health information. The ultimate goal of this effort is a nationwide health information network, which the lawmakers believed would improve patient care and reduce healthcare costs.

At the time these regulations were codified into law, the threats of cyber exploits where not well understood. As a result, the HIPAA Privacy Rule and other guidance by the U.S. Department of Health and Human Services (HHS) Office for Civil Rights (OCR) does not reference specific cyber-security safeguards, but rather merely requires providers to use their "best efforts" to protect the ePHI, which in the case of HIEs is contained in individuals' electronic health records (EHR). The protection of ePHI in the new information sharing environment mandated by the HITECH Act and other federal legislation is an imperative that comes essentially without a rule book.

Various organizations such as the Electronic Healthcare Network Accreditation Commission (EHNAC, www.EHNAC.org) and the California Association of Health Information Exchanges (www.ca-hie.org) have developed accreditation programs (HIEAP) and state-specific standards (CalDURSA) to provide guidance for the HIE's handling, transmission and exchange of electronic medical records. However, to date no national standard has emerged to provide a checklist audit to ensure that an HIE's software application and technology infrastructure are secure. This lack of specificity leaves many wondering if their electronic health records are "safe" in cloud-based portals managed by underfunded organizations which were chartered as a result of incentive-based programs—and are no longer receiving ongoing government funding.

Health Information Exchange Architecture

The HITECH Act established the HIE concept as a first step toward a national health information system. The concept was that regional healthcare organizations would work together on a local basis to establish methods for doctors, nurses and other healthcare providers to access and securely share a patient's vital medical information with an overall goal to improve the speed, quality and safety of patient care.

There are three types of health information exchange:

Directed exchange – provides the ability to send and receive secure information electronically between providers to support coordinated care;

Query-based exchange – gives providers the ability to find and/or request information on a patient from other providers. This method is often used for unplanned care such as automobile accidents and other emergency situations;

Consumer-mediated exchange – provides patients with the ability to aggregate and control the use of their health information among providers.

The regional HIE in this case study is a public exchange using the query-based exchange architecture. Each night, participant providers upload the key index fields from health records of patients who have authorized their participation in the program (via the HIPAA disclosure form) to a repository maintained by an external, third-party vendor using specialized software that is compatible with the major EHR systems. The records are transmitted using the HL7 message transport protocol which encrypts the data and ensures that the data does not "leak" during the transmission. It is important to note that the repository only contains index fields which facilitate the record search and not the entire health record.

In this architecture, the responsibilities for the Information Governance (IG) of the EHRs remain firmly with the organization which provided the medical service(s).

When a participant healthcare provider (doctor, nurse, ambulance driver) needs access to the patient's medical records, they utilize the HIE's web-portal to input demographic search criteria and query the repository. The repository software then queries the healthcare providers' database, packages a data stream in the HL7 format and sends it to the HIE's web server, which in turn decrypts the information and displays the health record information in a web browser for use by the requesting medical team. As a result of this process, the HIE facilitates the exchange, requesting and delivering the ePHI in encrypted format, but never storing the ePHI as data at rest.

NIST Cyber-security Framework

IG programs include many elements of operational business activities. One very important task is keeping data safe. Today, "safe" must be evaluated in the context of potential cyber-security threats. The charter to facilitate the exchange of ePHI in a secure environment brings with it the daunting responsibility to keep pace with bad actors who seek to compromise individual privacy for personal gain.

Executive Order #13636, Improving Critical Infrastructure Cybersecurity, was issued in 2013. This order directed the National Institute of Standards (NIST) to work with stakeholders to develop a voluntary framework based on existing standards, guidelines and practices for reducing cyber risks to critical infrastructure.

The NIST Cyber-security Framework outlines voluntary guidelines for enhancing corporate security posture. Although not mandated by regulation, the insurance industry is envisioned as the government's de facto enforcement arm, using the market tools of risk ratings and policy rates to drive U.S. companies into compliance with the NIST Cyber-security Framework guidelines. In addition, large accounting firms are starting to require both public and private businesses to engage third parties to perform vulnerability assessments of IT assets and corporate security posture. Soon, these assessments (mandated by auditors and suggested by insurance companies) will be expanded to include full compliance audits against the NIST Framework.

The security assessment performed for the HIE was aligned with the NIST Cyber-security Framework. The five elements of the NIST Framework are Identify, Protect, Detect, Respond and Recover, as depicted in the graphic below:

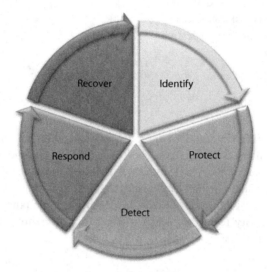

Utilizing the principles of the NIST Framework, the security team was able to assess the HIE's compliance with Framework guidelines and correspondingly its resilience to cyber-security threats. This approach is comprehensive and easy to understand:

- **Identify** by categorizing crown jewels and identifying risk areas
- **Protect** by safeguarding crown jewels and assets from data loss events
- **Detect** by spotting threats and non-compliance before it manifests into critical risk areas
- **Respond** by acting on incidents and activating plans to eradicate the threat and recover
- **Recover** by restoring critical capabilities based on pre-established plans and actions

HIE Security Assessment Project

HIPAA requires service providers who work with sub-contractors who have access to ePHI to enter into a business associates agreement (BAA). The BAA defines the healthcare service provider as a "covered entity" and the sub-contractor as a "business associate." The contractual wording in the BAA ensures that the regulatory obligations set forth in the Code of Federal Regulations (CFR) are clear and that provisions for potential data breaches and security incidents are established. The BAA also details the business associate's possible liabilities and the associated cyber-security insurance requirements.

In addition to the BAA, the security team worked with the HIE's staff to establish and authorize the Rules of Engagement (ROE) which detailed the systems that were in scope and the times during which the phishing campaigns, vulnerability scans and penetration tests could be performed. The ROE also specified the tools used on the project which included: Router Analysis Tool

(RAT), NMAP, Nessus, AppDetective AppScan, Critical watch FusionVM, Rapid7's Nexpose and Metasploit, Wireshark, Social Engineering Toolkit (SET), Burp Scanner and Kali ZAP Tools. The security assessment consisted of the following tasks:

- Internet footprint and attack surface
- Detailed website assessment (OWASP)
- Incident response testing and analysis
- Information security risk assessment
- Information technology risk assessment
- Social engineering
- Vulnerability assessment
- Penetration test
- HIPAA compliance audit

The Security Team utilized a standard approach to vulnerability assessments and penetration tests that is based on industry Best Practices. The Team used the methods defined by the Institute for Security and Open Methodologies (ISECOM). Their publication, the Open-Source Security Testing Methodology Manual (created by Pete Herzog, http://www.osstmm.org/), documents in great detail the components of a vendor-neutral approach to a wide range of assessment methods and techniques. The security team's approach to a security assessment and penetration testing includes the following elements:

Initiation: The project kick-off meeting introduced the teams, reviewed the project schedule and identified the actions necessary to formulate an agreement on the rules of engagement (ROE).

Discovery: Once the ROE was finalized and signed off, the first active step in the security assessment was to perform a discovery and footprint analysis of the network infrastructure. It is important to gain an understanding of what types of systems and services are present, as well as researching general information (such as contact names and DNS registration) available on the HIE and its websites from publicly available sources.

Initial assessment: The initial assessment included automated vulnerability and application scans of the HIE's systems. This information allowed the security team to have an understanding of operating system, application and service weaknesses that exist in the applications and infrastructure. The output from the automated scanning tools allowed the security team to quickly enumerate the potential issues.

Vulnerability analysis: The security team used the available information to identify vulnerabilities resulting from compound weakness across multiple systems. These included checking default passwords, validation of incorrect database configuration, enumeration of data available on external networks (such as through FTP and Windows File Share services) and other active exploitation techniques.

Exploitation: The security team exploited the network infrastructure within the (ROE). External black box penetration testing on systems simulated a real outside cyber threat. A gray box penetration test was then performed from inside the network to simulate a real insider cyber threat.

Reporting: The deliverables included both an executive summary of issues for management and detailed technical information for remediation tasks.

Lessons Learned

- The performance of an annual security assessment helps reduce risk to critical business assets by providing the HIE with a regular checkpoint to evaluate changes to systems and network infrastructure.
- The heat map risk chart provided the executive team with a visual representation of their cyber-security posture that was clear and easily understood. This allowed the vice president of operations to immediately prioritize remediation activities.
- The Internet footprint and attack surface analysis provided the CISO with graphical insights into operational issues which were subsequently remediated.
- The incident response testing identified response times which were outside the parameters of a vendor's service level agreement (SLA). As a result, the CISO was able to hold the vendor accountable and force them to meet the terms of the SLA.
- The information security risk assessment identified polices that were out of date and unavailable for employee review. In addition, there were controls that were not being audited for compliance on a regular basis.
- The information technology risk assessment identified threats that were previously unknown.
- The HIPAA compliance audit generated significant internal discussion, resulting in changes to internal procedures.

Security Assessment Findings

Overall, the HIE used best efforts to build usable systems and implement perimeter defenses to protect the core network from external attack. Some security gaps and software vulnerabilities were identified on internal systems. A remediation plan was presented that prioritized recommendations by severity and threat level.

The distributed architecture of the query-based exchange system provides an intrinsic level of cyber-security for the her, which minimizes or even negates the possibility that the HIE will expose data during normal data transmissions.

The IG responsibilities associated with the medical records remain with the organization that creates the medical record.

The medical professionals requesting the ePHI via the electronic exchange process have obligations under HIPAA and business associate agreements to safeguard the information during the time it is displayed on their computer systems. However, since the PHI is transitory and not stored locally, this risk is relatively small.

The human factor remains the weakest link in the HIE process. Compromised credentials and misuse by emergency personnel are human factors which represent significant risk, not only for the HIE in this case study, but all regional HIEs in general.

Security Assessment Best Practice Recommendations

Typically, cyber-security assessments are narrowly focused on the technical aspects of computer patching, network infrastructure and website programming. In this case, the security team's statement of work also included tasking to conduct an information security (IS) risk assessment and an information technology (IT) risk assessment. The IS assessment audited the HIE's posture relative to standard security controls. In addition, it also evaluated the HIE's compliance with its own set of policies and procedures. The IT assessment inventoried the HIE's computing infrastructure and then used a numerical system to model potential threats and score the associated risks.

The inclusion of the IS and IT risk assessments in the overall security assessment project scope delivered significant value to the HIE, bringing to light opportunities for improvement in the HIE's cyber-security posture that were not identified in the previous annual security assessment.

The security team recommended best practice is that all regional HIEs include information security risk assessment (controls audit) and information technology risk assessment (threat modeling) tasks in their annual security assessment projects.

Where Do You Keep Your Crown Jewels? Identifying, Classifying and Managing Your Information Assets

By Dennis Kessler

However we define it, the concept of "information management" has been around for many years, steadily growing as an industry and gaining in strategic importance for organizations, seemingly without much debate or controversy.

By contrast, information governance (IG), a relatively new upstart, can appear daunting.

The reason is that there is no single recipe for success. IG is not like an IT project, with a clear beginning, middle and end. Instead, it is more like a collection of complementary ongoing activities, all designed to improve the way we manage and secure information.

And all supported by some form of governance activity, checking whether we're moving in an agreed direction in terms of standards, guidelines and metrics.

Defining IG Isn't Hard

"Information governance" actually involves two distinct elements—instead of "governance over information," IG is really about *"governance over our information management activities."* It is about taking prudent care of information assets, minimizing their risks and costs while maximizing their value.

The National Archives of the U.K. government defines an information asset as "a body of information, defined and managed as a single unit so it can be understood, shared, protected and exploited effectively," adding that, "Information assets have recognizable and manageable value, risk, content and lifecycles."

The basic concept underpinning all information management and governance activities is the idea that information has value—and so needs to be managed and safeguarded accordingly based on its value.

Organizations manage their financial assets through a combination of policies, standards, systems and governance measures. These measures aim to achieve agreed levels of oversight, scrutiny and legal and regulatory compliance, while continuously improving.

In my experience, three key elements need to be in place for IG to flourish and deliver lasting benefits:

1. **Information principles**: These principles express the value of information and start to establish an information-focused culture in your organization.

    The principles might vary somewhat depending on the organization and industry. But they should include the following:

- **Information is a strategic asset of the organization**: All users recognize that information is essential for the organization to achieve its mission, objectives and activities.
- **Information belongs to the organization**: Even if an info asset has an accountable owner, it still exists to benefit the organization. The "owner" is more of a steward—managing the information to ensure its quality and availability to those who need it;
- **Information is controlled and managed**: Every information asset should be managed so that we know what information is stored where, how it is used, how important it is, etc.
- **Information is safeguarded**: According to a risk assessment of the value of the information. The more critical the information, the more stringent (and costly) should be the measures applied to protect it.
- **Information should be shared**: People must be able to find the information they need, when they need it.
- **Information has integrity**: Information owners and managers follow standards and measures to ensure that the information they're responsible for is trustworthy and accurate.
- **Information handling carries risks and responsibilities** for securing and properly utilizing information.

2. **Information standards, policies and guidelines**: For information management, which together describe specific behaviors, activities and outcomes needed to implement the principles and achieve the corresponding goals.
3. **Governance framework**: The structure of steering committees, roles and responsibilities and review processes which collectively asks, "How well are we meeting the principles?"

Measuring the Value of Information

In most organizations, requested spending on projects or operations requires a business case and projected "return on investment."

Although information is an asset, it's largely an intangible one, which means it's hard to put a firm dollar price on a piece or collection of information—at least in the traditional way accountants are trained to expect us to do.

Instead, think about the cost to operations, business process efficiency, customer trust and even reputation if the right information was not available to the right teams or systems at the right time.

This is exactly what information security is all about—and a good place to lay the solid foundations for effective information management and governance—even if we are unable to fund and launch a formal explicit IG program.

Although recognition of the value of IG is slowly growing, information security and, specifically, "cyber-security" are now firmly on the table as agenda items for executive boards around the world. Indeed, given the widespread recent publicity resulting from industrial-scale data breaches at Anthem, 21st Century Oncology, Sony, Target and even the U.S. Office of Personnel Management.

Information security is now seen as an existential threat to some organizations and even economic growth (according to the World Economic Forum).

Locating the "Crown Jewels"—and Protecting Them

Once we have located an information asset, we you need to analyze and classify it to build a simple profile. We will then store and maintain the profiles in an **information asset register**.

The term "information security" is based on the idea that information represents an asset which has a value.

To determine the criticality of an asset, we consider the impact of loss of the asset's:

- **Confidentiality**: Has there been a breach of unauthorized access?
- **Integrity**: Can we trust the information to be accurate and complete? Has the information been tampered with or corrupted?
- **Availability**: Is the information available to those people, processes or systems who need it, when they need it?

Based on its resulting criticality value, each information asset needs a corresponding level of protection—specifically, to safeguard and maintain its availability, confidentiality and integrity.

The resulting criticality value then suggests the corresponding level of protection needed to safeguard and maintain its availability, confidentiality and integrity.

Benefits of Tracking Your Information Assets

As well as greater confidence that you are protecting your information assets appropriately, this asset-based approach to managing information helps to reveal:

- Which people or teams are responsible and accountable for maintaining the confidentiality, integrity and availability of information
- Which people/teams and systems can access information, and for what purposes—whether to create, update or consume information
- How information flows and is used throughout the organization—which business processes and which decision-making points depend on which information
- Regulatory, compliance and other obligations

General Regulation on Data Protection (GDPR) Considerations

U.S. healthcare organizations are already familiar with the need to comply with the Health Insurance Portability and Accountability Act (HIPAA), the U.S. law requiring protection of confidential and sensitive patient data.

The regulatory burden can be significant. As well as complying with HIPAA, from May 2018 healthcare companies in Europe or doing business with European citizens also have to meet the conditions of the EU General Regulation on Data Protection (GDPR). The GDPR is perhaps the most strict privacy regulation to date. Its effects are being felt around the globe, and it will most likely influence a tightening of U.S. privacy laws.

To stay on the right side of GDPR, it is essential to discover and document what personal data you hold (irrespective of whether it is for patients, staff or suppliers), where it came from, how you use it and why, and who you share it with. And the only way to get a reliable picture of the situation is to carry out an information audit.

Other activities which organizations must carry out to comply with these regulations include ensuring:

- privacy notices and policies are aligned with the regulations, such as the specific purpose(s) for which data is stored and processed

- individuals' rights, including procedures to support requests for data retrieval and deletion
- data is stored securely and appropriately given its sensitivity

Achieving all of these and other related points depends on understanding what data you're storing, where you're storing it and what is represents.

As is generally true for all customer data, the mining and analysis of patient data can be the key to innovation and big profits for healthcare companies. However, managing this precious patient and customer data means balancing the potential rewards with privacy responsibilities and costs. Customers and patients are increasingly aware, empowered and concerned with privacy.

Sample Information Asset Survey Questions

1. **Information Asset Description**
   a. **Name**: A descriptive and meaningful label for the asset
   b. **Description**: What is the information asset and what it is used for
2. **Ownership**: This section covers the "stewardship" of the information asset, including the key roles and responsibilities of the owner and manager, together with any other stakeholders likely to be affected by the quality and availability of the asset
   a. **Owner** has overall accountability for access, use and management of the asset
   b. **Manager**: Hands-on manager responsible for day-to-day operations and administration. Expected to be familiar with the details of the asset content, structure and usage, and so likely to be quick to detect evidence of breach, tampering/corruption etc.
   c. **Creator**: Source of the information; a person, application system or external source
   d. **Stakeholders/Customers**: Other stakeholders affected by the use, management, integrity or availability of the asset
3. **Dates**
   a. **Creation date**: Date on which the asset was created (if involving a fixed lifecycle)
   b. **Last review date**: Date on which the asset was last reviewed for completeness and accuracy
   c. **Date closed**: Date on which the asset was closed/completed/removed from production use
4. **Confidentiality**
   a. **Confidentiality**: Indicates the confidentiality classification of the information based on the BIS Confidentiality of Information policy (SN 1045) (NB this is distinct from the **Risk/Impact Criticality** rating in section 7 below.)
   b. **Data Privacy and Protection**: Indicates whether the asset contains or relates to Personally Identifiable Information (PII) and potential relevance to Data Protection or Data Privacy regulations and legal risk—especially the EU General Data Protection Regulation (GDPR).
5. **Retention**
   a. **Retention period**: Retention category (if useful—but avoid duplication and inconsistency)
   b. **System of Record**: Name of the record system used to store the asset (or a subset of related business records)
6. **Access and Use**
   a. **Applications and Interfaces**: List of applications and interfaces authorized to access the information asset, together with the corresponding access rights
   b. **User groups**: List of user groups authorized to access the asset, together with the corresponding access rights
   c. **Metadata**: List of any metadata needed to access or describe the context of the asset

7. **Risk/Impact of Problems/Issues**
   a. **Confidentiality**: Impact if the asset is accessed or disclosed without authorization
   b. **Integrity**: Impact if the information is corrupted, tampered with or otherwise suffers a loss of integrity
   c. **Availability**: Impact if the information is lost or unavailable
   d. **Criticality**: The overall criticality rating is the product of the combined scores of the above confidentiality, integrity and availability ratings.

25 Exciting Things to Do with an Information Asset Register

By Reynold Leming

Many organizations have undertaken information audits to gain an insight to this highly valuable corporate asset. This is particularly the case for those who will be governed by the EU General Data Protection Regulation, where there are increased obligations to maintain documentary evidence of processing activities. However, there are of course many drivers for understanding the information assets maintained and used, their characteristics and the value and risks associated with them.

Whether in a spreadsheet form or (ideally) a database, an information asset register (IAR) is used to record the inventory. This chapter explores (in no particular order of importance) 25 potentially beneficial outcomes from populating, maintaining and interrogating an IAR:

1. **Understanding relationships**: A related series of records sharing the same purpose (an "asset collection" if you will) might have a variety of constituent entities ("assets") in different formats – e.g. physical records, digital content, system data. Identifying these within an IAR, with a suitable narrative recorded, will enable an understanding of their relationships and purpose over time. This could include for example the "story" of document handling paper originals and resulting images within a document scanning process or the retirement and introduction of systems.

   Allied to this is tagging assets to a business classification scheme of the functions and activities of your organization. This allows the assets to be categorized to a vocabulary of business activity that is neutral to and more stable than organizational structures (which can change more often than what an organization actually does), provides a collated corporate view of assets maintained based upon their purpose (for example many departments will hold invoice, staff, policy and contract records) and supports cross-cutting processes involving different teams. It also allows the consistent inheritance and application of business rules, such as retention policies.

2. **Security classification**: Assets can be classified within the IAR to an approved security classification/protective marking scheme, with current protective measures recorded, in order to identify if there are in any risks relating to the handling of confidential personal or commercially sensitive information. You can assess that assets are handled, stored, transferred and disposed of in an appropriate manner.

3. **Personal data**: Specifically, you can identify confidential personal information to ensure that data protection and privacy obligations are met.

   The GDPR contains many obligations that require a thorough understanding of what personal data you process and how and why you do so. Many requirements for keeping records as a Data Controller for GDPR Article 30 can be supported by the information asset inventory. For example, the asset attributes can describe the purposes of the processing, the categories of data subjects and personal data, categories of recipients, envisaged time limits for erasure of the different categories of data and a general description of the technical and organizational security measures.

It will also help data processors keep a record of the categories of processing, transfers of personal data to a third country or an international organization and a general description of the technical and organizational security measures.

Much of the information about personal data required for Article 30 compliance is also useful to meet obligations under Article 13 and Article 14 on information to be provided, for example via privacy notices or consent forms.

Under Chapter 3 of the GDPR, data subjects have a number of rights. Understanding things such as the location, format, use of and lawful basis of processing for different categories of personal data will enable support responses to rights and requests.

Under Article 25 of the GDPR there are requirements for Data Protection by design and by default. Additionally, under Article 35 there are requirements relating to Data Protection impact assessments. The inventory can provide insight to which processes and systems need to be assessed based upon for example the nature, scope, context and purposes of processing as well as the risks of varying likelihood and severity for rights and freedoms of natural persons posed by the processing.

As aforementioned, it is important to identify who personal data is shared with. The inventory can support this as well as specifically enable monitoring of the existence or status or suitable agreements. For example under Article 28 of the GDPR processing by a processor shall be governed by a contract or other legal act under Union or Member State law.

Article 32 of the GDPR covers security of processing, with requirements to implement appropriate technical and organizational measures to ensure a level of security appropriate to the risk. Then using the inventory you can assess the security measures in place for assets against their level of confidentiality. It also can help with identifying the data sets where, if anything unfortunate were to happen, there are considerations regarding Article 33 Notification of a personal data breach to the supervisory authority and Article 34 Communication of a personal data breach to the data subject.

4. **Ownership**: The ability to know: Who owns what? This includes understanding ownership both in terms of corporate accountability and ownership of the actual information itself. You could also record who administers an asset on a day-to-day basis if this is different.

5. **Business continuity**: An organization will have vital/business-critical records that are necessary for it to continue to operate in the event of a disaster. They include those records which are required to recreate the organization's legal and financial status, to preserve its rights, and to ensure that it can continue to fulfill its obligations to its stakeholders. Assets can be classified within the IAR to an approved criticality classification scheme, with current protective measures recorded, in order to assess whether they are stored and protected in a suitable manner and identify if there are in any risks relating to business-critical ("vital record") information. You can also identify the recovery point objective (RPO) and recovery time objective (RTO) for assets to support a disaster recovery or data protection plan.

6. **Originality**: You can identify whether an asset is original or a copy, ascertaining its relative importance and supporting decisions on removing duplication and the optimization of business processes.

7. **Heritage**: You can identify records of historical importance that can be transferred at some stage to the custody of a corporate or third-party archive.

8. **Formats**: The ability to understand the formats used for information, supporting decisions on digital preservation or migration.

9. **Space planning**: In order to support office moves and changes, data can be gathered for physical assets relating to their volume, footprint, rate of accumulation, use, filing methods etc.

10. **Subject matter**: If assets are tagged to a business classification scheme of functions and activities, as well potentially to a keyword list, the organization can understand the "spread" of record types (e.g. who holds personnel, financial, contractual records) and/or "discover" resources for knowledge management or eDiscovery purposes.

11. **Archive management**: The ability to understand what physical records (paper, backup tapes, etc.) are archived, where and when; this might for example identify risks in specific locations or issues with the regularity of archiving processes. The organization can also understand its utilization of third-party archive storage vendors—potentially supporting decisions on contract management/consolidation—and maintain their own future-proof inventory of archive holdings. Archive transactions can be recorded if there is no system to otherwise do so.

12. **Location**: The "location" of an asset can of course be virtual or physical. This (together with other questions relating to for example security measures) is important to ensure that information assets are suitably protected. It also helps in the planning of IT systems and physical filing/archiving services. The benefits for archive management are explored above and for maintaining a system catalogue below. Other examples might be to identify records to gather when doing an office sweep following vacation of a floor or building, or what assets are held in the cloud, or asset types within a given jurisdiction. It would also support the "discovery" of resources for knowledge management or eDiscovery purposes.

13. **Retention**: An IAR can be used both to link assets with approved records retention policies and understand the policies and methods currently applied within the organization, therefore identifying queries, risks and issues. The IAR can also be used to maintain the actual policies (across jurisdictions if applicable) and their citations; if a law changes or is enacted, relevant assets can be identified for any process changes to be made.

14. **Disposal**: An IAR can be used both to link assets with approved destruction or transfer policies and understand the processes and methods currently applied within the organization, therefore identifying queries, risks and issues, particularly for confidential information. Disposal transactions can be recorded if there is no system to otherwise do so.

15. **Source**: The source of assets can be identified to understand where information is derived from and better manage the information supply chain. Under Article 14 of the GDPR, part of the information the controller shall provide to the data subject to ensure fair and transparent processing includes from which source the personal data originated, and if applicable, whether it came from publicly accessible sources.

16. **Rights**: The rights held in and over assets can be identified, such as copyright and intellectual property, in order to protect IPR and to avoid infringement of the rights of others.

17. **Applications catalogue**: The application systems in use (e.g. content management, front and back office) can be identified and be linked in locations, people, activities and of course assets. Licensing and upgrade criteria could also be managed. It would also be possible for example to identify system duplication or the use of homegrown databases.

18. **Condition**: Both physical and digital assets can degrade; this can be identified for assets with conservation/preservation actions taken accordingly.

19. **Age**: The age of assets can be established, with decisions made on their further retention/ disposal, the need for archiving (historic or business) and potentially whether they need to be superseded with newer resources.

20. **Organization and Referencing**: An understanding can be gained of whether structured systems and approaches are in place to describe, reference and organize physical and digital assets, identifying if there are likely to be any issues with the finding information.

21. **Utilization**: An understanding can be gained of whether assets are proposed, active, inactive, discontinued/superseded, therefore enabling decisions on their format, storage, disposal, etc.

22. **Sharing**: An IAR can be used to identify how information is shared within and without the organization, helping ensure that it is available as required, and that suitable security measures and, where applicable, information sharing agreements are in place. This supports compliance with Article 30 of the GDPR as part of the records of processing activities.

23. **Provenance**: Fundamentally an IAR can provide an accountable audit trail of asset existence and activity, including any changes in ownership and custody of the resource since its creation that are significant for its authenticity, integrity and interpretation.

24. **Publications**: Information produced for wider publication to an internal or external resource can be identified, including for example the audience for whom the resource is intended or useful, the channels used for distribution and the language(s) of the content, thus facilitating editorial, production and dissemination planning and management.

25. **Quality**: Observations can be recorded on the quality of assets (e.g. accuracy, completeness, reliability, relevance, consistency across data sources, accessibility), with risks and issues identified and managed.

Privacy and Data Protection Officers: Implementing the EU General Data Protection Regulation

By Andrew Harvey and Barry Moult

Introduction

At time of writing the European Union General Data Protection Regulation (GDPR) is being subsumed into British domestic legislation, and will become the basis for a new Data Protection Act, replacing the old 1998 Act, itself based on a 1995 EU Directive. For this reason, until the new Act receives Royal Assent, this piece continues to refer to the GDPR. The pending legislation is, overall, causing much generalized debate regarding its implications and where Data Protection practice in the U.K. is destined.

There has been substantial specific debate and concern about who should be appointed as the Data Protection Officer (DPO) under the GDPR within healthcare organisations. In this section we will attempt to inject some order into the confusion. This has concentrated on the GDPR itself, along with guidance from the Article 29 Working Group (WP29), the U.K. Information Commissioner's Office's (ICO), and significant discussion between the authors, both interpersonally and online with Information Governance (IG) and Data Protection professionals.

The perspective here is mostly applicable to Acute trusts within the National Health Service (NHS), although its message is likely to be applicable more broadly across the U.K. healthcare sector.

Is a DPO Required?

GDPR Article 37 states that a DPO is needed in any case where:

■ The processing is carried out by a public authority or body, except for courts, or
■ The core activities of the Data Controller or the Data Processor consist of processing operations which, by virtue of their nature, their scope and/or their purposes, require regular and systematic monitoring of data subjects on a large scale, or
■ The core activities of the Data Controller or the Data Processor consist of processing large volumes of Special Categories of Data or information about criminal convictions and offences.[1]

Whereas it is common understanding that the NHS is a public body, the term "public authority or body" is, rather unhelpfully, not defined in the GDPR. For sake of clarity, however, it is apparent by extrapolation from the definition in Schedule 1 of the Freedom of Information Act 2000, that the NHS is indeed included.

Who Should Be the DPO?

It is perfectly acceptable for public bodies to appoint a single DPO to be shared between authorities.[2] It may be beneficial, therefore, that the DPO is shared between healthcare organizations working in close partnership with each other, or perhaps across several organizations within a localized Sustainability and Transformation Partnership, Accountable Care Organization/Partnership or other similar forms of partnership working.

GDPR Article 38 is clear about the position of the DPO, in that the Data Controller and Data Processor shall:

■ Ensure that the DPO is involved, properly and in a timely manner, in all issues which relate to the protection of personal data.
■ Support the DPO in performing their tasks by providing resources necessary to carry out those tasks and access to personal data and processing operations, and to maintain their expert knowledge.
■ Ensure that the DPO does not receive any instructions regarding the exercise of those tasks. He or she shall not be dismissed or penalized by the Data Controller or the Data Processor for performing his tasks. The DPO shall report to the highest management level.[3]

Furthermore:

■ Data Subjects may contact the DPO with regard to all issues related to processing of their personal data and to the exercise of their rights under the GDPR.
■ The DPO shall be bound by secrecy or confidentiality concerning the performance of his or her tasks.
■ The DPO may fulfill other tasks and duties. The Data Controller or Data Processor shall ensure that any such tasks and duties do not result in a conflict of interests.[4]

With regard to the last point, WP29 clarifies that:

As a rule of thumb, conflicting positions within the organisation may include senior management positions (such as chief executive, chief operating, chief financial, chief medical officer, head of marketing department, head of Human Resources or head of IT departments) but also other roles lower down in the organisational structure if such positions or roles lead to the determination of purposes and means of processing. In addition, a conflict of interests may also arise for example if an external DPO is asked to represent the controller or processor before the Courts in cases involving data protection issues.[5]

DPOs do not have to be lawyers but need expert knowledge of Data Protection law and practices. From a practical perspective, they must also have an excellent understanding of the organization's governance structure and be familiar with its IT infrastructure and technology.

The DPO role may be employed ("internal DPO"), or there may be circumstances were they may act under a service contract ("external DPO"). In both cases, they must be given the necessary resources to fulfill the relevant job functions and be granted a certain level of independence, to be able to act in the necessary 'independent manner'. This independence is supported by a degree of protection against dismissal or other sanctions on grounds that relate to their performance of their DPO tasks.

The DPO does not have to be a standalone role, and may have other tasks within the organization, so long as they do not interfere with the DPO role. WP29 has made it clear that the DPO 'cannot hold a position within the organization that leads him or her to determine the purposes and the means of the processing of personal data'.[6] For example, it is the responsibility of the Data Controller or Data Processor to maintain a record of processing operations under its responsibility or maintain a record of all categories of processing activities carried out on behalf of a Data Controller. In reality, however, it may be the DPO that creates the inventories and holds the register of processing operations even though it is not a specific requirement of the role.

Many healthcare organizations already have staff in place who oversees most issues relating to Data Protection. These roles generally have titles such as Head of IG, IG Lead, IG Manager or Privacy Officer. It is anticipated that it is these roles that will be most appropriate to undertaking the DPO role within healthcare organizations with mature IG models as it is these personnel who have the necessary IG and Data Protection knowledge and experience to undertake the role.

To make this appropriate, the addition of the DPO post to such roles will require both an amendment to the post holder's Job Description, including an appropriately senior salary band/grading, along with a clear reporting responsibility (a dotted line in some circumstances) to a Director, Executive Director and/or Board member, depending on the structure, size and maturity of the organization.

What Are the Qualifications to Be a DPO?

GDPR Article 37 does not absolutely define the credentials for a DPO beyond 'expert knowledge of data protection law and practices'.[7] The GDPR's Recitals add that this should be 'determined in particular according to the data processing operations carried out and the protection required for the personal data processed by the controller or the processor'.[8]

Realistically this is a member of staff with detailed expert knowledge and experience of applying IG and Data Protection principles within a healthcare environment, potentially along with a qualification to demonstrate the ability to act at this level.

The WP29 guidance clarifies this further:

Although Article 37(5) does not specify the professional qualities that should be considered when designating the DPO, it is a relevant element that DPOs should have expertise in national and European data protection laws and practices and an in-depth understanding of the GDPR. It is also helpful if the supervisory authorities promote adequate and regular training for DPOs.

Knowledge of the business sector and of the organization of the controller is useful. The DPO should also have sufficient understanding of the processing operations carried out, as well as the information systems, and data security and data protection needs of the controller.

In the case of a public authority or body, the DPO should also have a sound knowledge of the administrative rules and procedures of the organization.[9]

What Are the Tasks of the DPO?

The DPO's tasks are very clearly delineated in the GDPR Article 39, to:

■ Inform and advise the Data Controller or Data Processor and the employees who carry out processing of their Data Protection obligations.
■ Monitor Data Protection compliance.
■ Assign responsibilities, awareness-raising and training of staff involved in processing operations.
■ Undertake internal audits of Data Protection.
■ Provide advice on the need and completion of Data Protection Impact Assessments.
■ Cooperate with the ICO and act as the contact point for any issues relating to processing.
■ Undertake or advise on the potential risk of processing activities.

Under the GDPR, DPOs have many rights in addition to their responsibilities; they:

■ May insist upon resources to fulfill their job functions and for their own ongoing training.
■ Must have access to the company's Data Processing personnel and operations.
■ Have significant independence in the performance of their roles.
■ Have a reporting line 'to the highest management level' of the organization.

What Are the Organization's Responsibilities?

The most essential requirement is that the DPO must be allowed to perform their tasks in an independent manner. They need to report to the highest management level in the organization and cannot be dismissed or penalized for doing their job (i.e. giving advice). This will require a robust governance reporting structure for the DPO to function and evidence that advice has been accepted or rejected.

GDPR Article 38 requires the organization to support its DPO by 'providing resources necessary to carry out [their] tasks and access to personal data and processing operations, and to maintain his or her expert knowledge'. The WP29 Guidance adds that, depending on the nature of the processing operations and the activities and size of the organization, the following resources should be provided to the DPO:

■ *Active support of the DPO's function by senior management (such as at board level).*
■ *Sufficient time for DPOs to fulfil their duties. This is particularly important where the DPO is appointed on a part-time basis or where the employee carries out data protection in addition to*

other duties. Otherwise, conflicting priorities could result in the DPO's duties being neglected. Having sufficient time to devote to DPO tasks is paramount. It is a good practice to establish a percentage of time for the DPO function where it is not performed on a full-time basis. It is also good practice to determine the time needed to carry out the function, the appropriate level of priority for DPO duties, and for the DPO (or the organization) to draw up a work plan.

■ *Adequate support in terms of financial resources, infrastructure (premises, facilities, equipment) and staff where appropriate.*

■ *Official communication of the designation of the DPO to all staff to ensure that their existence and function is known within the organization.*

■ *Necessary access to other services, such as Human Resources, legal, IT, security, etc., so that DPOs can receive essential support, input and information from those other services.*

■ *Continuous training. DPOs should be given the opportunity to stay up to date with regard to developments within data protection. The aim should be to constantly increase the level of expertise of DPOs and they should be encouraged to participate in training courses on data protection and other forms of professional development, such as participation in privacy fora, workshops, etc.*

■ *Given the size and structure of the organization, it may be necessary to set up a DPO team (a DPO and his/her staff). In such cases, the internal structure of the team and the tasks and responsibilities of each of its members should be clearly drawn up. Similarly, when the function of the DPO is exercised by an external service provider, a team of individuals working for that entity may effectively carry out the tasks of a DPO as a team, under the responsibility of a designated lead contact for the client.*[10]

Failure to appoint a DPO where required can lead to significant ramifications. Administrative fines can be as high as the equivalent of €10m (almost £9m at time of writing) or 2% of the organization's turnover, whichever is higher.

The appointment of a DPO may look unnecessary at first ("we already have an IG Manager"). However, not only is it a legal requirement, it must also be seen as an efficient way to ensure Data Protection compliance, something that is especially true when it comes to sophisticated Data Processing activities and cross-border data flows.

What Could a DPO Job Description Look Like?

By nature of being different organizations, operating in their own way, these will likely vary widely across healthcare. Some organizations may opt for an addition to the Job Description of the member of staff completing the role that is as simple as 'To act as the Trust's responsible Data Protection Officer, as defined in the General Data Protection Regulation' (as is the case with one of the authors). Others may desire something more detailed. A possible example is as follows:

Job Description

DATA PROTECTION OFFICER

1. ROLE PURPOSE

The Purpose of the Data Protection Officer (DPO) is to provide the organization independent risk-based advice to support its decision-making in the appropriateness of processing Personal and Special Categories of Data within the Principles and Data Subject Rights laid down in the General Data Protection Regulation (GDPR).

2. TASKS

Within the GDPR, the DPO's tasks are summarized as:

- Leading from the front in promoting an appropriate Data Protection culture within the organization.
- Setting organizational trigger-points for mandatory input from the DPO.
- Close liaison with senior clinical and nonclinical colleagues to enable and support both operational and strategic decision-making.
- Management of a governance structure to record Data Protection decisions made by the organization.
- Provision of advice on complex Data Protection issues, such as Subject Access Requests, procurement decisions, Information/Cyber Security and Information Sharing.
- Sign-off of regulatory requirements, e.g. Information Governance Toolkit submissions.
- Maintaining ongoing personal development and knowledge of Data Protection law, issues and developments.
- Informing and advising the organization and its staff about their obligations to comply with the GDPR and other Data Protection laws.
- Monitoring compliance with the GDPR and other Data Protection laws, including:
- Managing internal Data Protection activities.
- Advising on Data Protection Impact Assessments.
- Training staff.
- Conducting internal audits.
- Being the first point of contact for the Information Commissioner's Office and/or Data Subjects.

3. PERSON SPECIFICATION

- Demonstrable expert knowledge of Data Protection law and practices, gained by formal qualification and/or experience.
- In-depth knowledge and practical experience of the NHS.
- Confidence, although employed by the organization, to act "as if" independent, especially when liaising with senior colleagues.
- The equivalent seniority of Band 8a or above.[11]

Long-Term Digital Preservation in IG Programs: Advice from the Pharmaceutical and Biotechnology World

By Patricia Morris and Lori J. Ashley

Introduction

Pharmaceutical and biotechnology companies have numerous compelling use cases for long-term digital archiving and preservation capabilities for their information and records. Research, development, and manufacturing processes that bring products to market are complex, decades in duration, and subject to health authority regulatory and industry standards. With only minor exceptions, information and records generated during drug development are now managed exclusively in digitally encoded formats. Additionally, with its close alliance to healthcare organizations during the clinical phase of drug development, there are common directives between these industries for the compliant management of protected health information (PHI), personally identifiable information (PII), and confidential or sensitive information.

A significant percentage of information assets created and used in the pharmaceutical and bio-technology industries require long-term retention and access in excess of 10 years. The information must be able to survive successive generations of technology and custodians with all the necessary controls in place to assure it is protected. It is imperative that Information Technology (IT) professionals have strategies and capabilities to address this demand to ensure that these mission-critical organizational and customer information assets are managed appropriately with integrity and security maintained and availability assured for their lifespans.

The Challenges of Long-Term Digital Preservation in Information Governance

First of all, what does "long-term" mean?

- Long enough to be concerned with the impacts of changing technologies, including support for new media and data formats, or with a changing user community. Long term may extend indefinitely, but may start in as soon as 10 years.

Digital information with retention periods of 10 years or more must remain protected, usable, retrievable, and authentic over successive generations. Hence, digital preservation is defined as:

- The long-term, secure, and error-free storage of digital information, with means for retrieval and interpretation, for the entire lifespan the information is required to be retained.

This is a challenge because digital content is fragile and dependent on ever-changing hardware and software to be readable and usable. Risks to maintaining the integrity and authenticity of digital information over time include:

- Limited budgets
- Lack of specialized expertise
- Insufficient or outdated technical infrastructure
- Mismanagement or loss of materials while in the hands of the creators
- Lack of descriptive information or sufficient metadata
- Bit rot or other forms of media corruption
- Unreadable file formats
- Human error
- Lack of specialized technical expertise
- Unintended information security breaches

Building a long-term digital preservation solution, or electronic archive (eArchive) requires investment by the organization for this new process and technology. Justifying the costs and building the right business case for the eArchive is an essential part of an overall IG strategy. Different stakeholders in the organization will have views on the drivers for such an investment. Their views are likely derived from what they are accountable for in their role and how their budgets are defined and justified. Their drivers may come from expected compliance to external laws and regulations or from directives regarding costs savings and efficiency, or both. In the following case study, the principals in the project were primarily driven by their need to show compliance to regulations stipulated by health authorities in numerous national jurisdictions.

Case Study

This is a description of the process used by a pharmaceutical company to establish a digital archive for electronic study records and data generated during the Pre-Clinical Research phase of drug development.

The digital information identified for preservation and storage in the Pharma eArchive is subject to regulations issued by health authorities, as well as relevant laws pertaining to electronic recordkeeping. Strict compliance with these laws and regulations is essential to company operations and is routinely audited for assurance. In this instance, compliance with a specific set of regulations from the United States Food and Drug Administration (U.S. FDA) Code of Federal Regulations (CFR) that define archiving practices for records created according to Good Laboratory Practice (GLP) was the primary driver for the development of the eArchive. These essential business records have significant value to the Company in terms of scientific innovation and evidence, and are commonly retained in excess of 50 years.

Project Approach

The scope of the eArchive project was to determine a technology solution to support long-term preservation and management of electronic Pre-Clinical GLP records and data sets. This effort was undertaken with the understanding that business processes, roles and responsibilities, workflows and technology must work in concert to cover the entire spectrum of required capabilities and lifespan controls defined by the future users of the solution. To that end, a cross-functional team was convened which included Pre-Clinical scientists, Quality Managers, and Information Technologists. External consultants, who were experts in delivering long-term digital preservation and pharmaceutical electronic archiving solutions, supported the team. This collaboration resulted in the development of a formal set of user requirements and technical specifications for the eArchive.

Initially, there was an emphasis on finding a solution for the long-term preservation of structured and proprietary data sets. Demonstrations of six solutions were conducted to stimulate project team discussion and ensure that user requirements for the GLP eArchive would meet future operational and compliance demands. The solutions reviewed ranged from full-blown enterprise records and content management solutions to database archiving to long-term digital preservation systems. As a result of the demonstrations and an additional review of the full requirements it was determined that more than one technology solution may ultimately be required to address the full spectrum of content types (structured, semi-structured, and unstructured information).

The external consultants developed an initial eArchive Operating Model so the project team could envision the process of how records would be appraised, ingested and archived. The basis of this model was the approach defined in ISO 14721:2012 (a Space data and information transfer systems – Open archival information system (OAIS) – Reference model) with customizations based on internal process demands. The model showed the records moving from production systems, through appraisal and preparation for ingest, long-term management and storage in the eArchive (including file format transformations when necessary), subsequent search and retrieval, as well as potential disposition. At this point, the project team produced the final set of user requirements for the solution.

As a result of this newly confirmed focus and adjustment to the project scope and user requirements, a formal request for proposal (RFP) was issued to the two long-term digital preservation system vendors who had demonstrated the highest degree of capability for the required ingest and lifespan management capabilities for the eArchive.

The outcome of the RFP process was that a preferred vendor was selected to fulfill project requirements. A three-month Proof of Concept (POC) project using a cloud-based version was completed and the results confirmed the suitability of the solution.

Project Results

Following the POC and based on new technical and legal requirements, the Company made a software selection for their final solution. The software is a modular on-premise preservation platform that will be configured and customized to meet Company needs. The Company's central IT will manage the repository and the archival content storage will be based on the Company's Amazon S3 account. The logical architecture is a standard three-tier web-application architecture. The presentation tier (access interface) is primarily a web interface serving a combination of static and dynamic HTML pages. The application tier is a series of Java-based applications, using J2EE standards. The relational database will be based on MS SQL and hosted internally.

The categories of records to be ingested was expanded after the POC to include other research and development (R&D) groups. The Company launched the next phase of the project and it was understood that in order to maintain compliance to applicable external regulations, the solution would need to be fully validated against the approved user requirements and technical specifications (as well as internal Information Technology Validation standards). So effort was put toward finalizing those documents. Work was undertaken in parallel to revise and update records transfer and archiving processes and the associated roles and responsibilities within the record creating units. The end result delivers their new way of preserving essential electronic drug development records for the long term with the expectation that compliance requirements will be met.

Case Study Summary

It is well established that a vast amount of digital information is generated in the healthcare industry and some of it must be retained and remain viable for a very long time, often in complex or proprietary file formats and outside of the systems in which it was generated. The need for companies and institutions in the healthcare arena to devise and implement a long-term digital preservation strategy and solution as part of their overall IG program is essential. It will ensure that the digital information with long-term preservation requirements will remain protected, usable, retrievable, and authentic over successive generations. Implementing a true eArchive solution, with appropriate controls and systems in place for digital preservation, will provide the secure and error-free storage environment with the means for retrieval and interpretation, for the entire lifespan the information is required to be retained.

Building the Business Case for Digital Preservation

Compliance: The case study summarizes a project whose justification was based on the need for compliance to laws and regulations related to use of electronic information systems for creating and managing information that has long-term retention and reuse requirements. The demand and funding for the project was raised by those in the company who were accountable for assuring that compliance through their Quality Management Framework and corporate Code of Conduct.

Cost savings: Another driver for justifying the investment in an eArchive solution can be derived through the decommissioning of information systems that are no longer actively being used but remain online to retain their content due to retention obligations. The proper eArchive solution will assure the integrity and availability of the information, independent of the originating system, for the lifespan of the content. This will allow for the decommissioning of applications and can provide an equivalent or greater cost savings than the cost to build and maintain the eArchive itself. Those within IT know that while storage may be inexpensive, the overall application infrastructure and human resources required to manage it is not.

Value Protection: A mature IG program will also uncover a likely significant quantity of information that is being retained well past its usefulness or obligation (as defined in the organization's records management policy and retention schedule). While searching for the "gems" that require long-term digital preservation within the enterprise to be ingested into an eArchive, a lot of redundant, outdated, and trivial (ROT) information will be identified that can be disposed of to free up existing storage, assure compliance to internal policies, and potentially reduce future eDiscovery costs. A business case that calculates all of these factors and projects the future escalation of costs and risks without action will justify the investment in an eArchive that will assure long-term digital preservation.

IG Education Is Key to Success

By Robert F. Smallwood

Usually, securing budget for any project or program is the primary obstacle to moving forward. That is not the case with information governance (IG) programs, according to IG practitioners.

The leading barriers to success in IG programs are education, program communications, and executive sponsorship.

Lack of understanding and awareness of the value of IG is often cited by practitioners. This can be remedied at a modest cost with IG training courses, webinars, podcasts, books, and articles. (Go to www.IGTraining.com for options.)

Other major barriers to IG progress are rather "soft" skills, that is lack of collaboration across functional groups, change management, and planning. These challenges can also be overcome mostly with focused directives and an investment of time, prior to undertaking the IG program effort in earnest.

IG is a complex undertaking that requires cross-functional collaboration. And for IG programs to launch, a wide net must be cast. IG programs must have support from core IG-related functions, including legal, IT, information security, and health information management (HIM). But a particular IG program can span across many more functional groups, including data privacy, compliance, human resources, analytics, audit, finance, and business units, according to an article published by Baron and Marcos in the October/November 2015 issue of *Practical Law*. We would add risk management and possibly knowledge management to this list. Bear in mind that IG programs must be customized to meet the business objectives of specific organizations.

With significant roles from such varied functions required for IG program success, it stands to reason that they must have a common understanding of IG, a common language—its key terms, its benefits, and how the IG program will contribute to the accomplishment of the healthcare enterprise's business objectives. This means your IG team or steering committee must have baseline IG training to give the program a chance at succeeding.

It also means that close attention must be paid to communication and change management factors, which should be intertwined with IG training efforts to reinforce and support program objectives.

IG Insight: The Soft Stuff Is the Hard Stuff

By Robert F. Smallwood

When organizations seek out answers for the keys to success in IG programs, they often get the typical answer from consultants and vendors: it depends.

Sure, it depends on the focus of the initial effort in an IG program. The business driver for some organizations may be cost-cutting measures that focus on reducing redundant, outdated, and trivial (ROT) files to cut the cost of storage, or at least abate it.

Hard dollar savings can be made by reducing storage costs of central servers while additional savings can be gained through improved content organization (through improved taxonomy design and leveraging metadata) which lowers e-discovery collection and document review costs. That's "hard" stuff that yields hard dollar cost savings, but it is relatively straightforward. Further, search capabilities on unstructured files such as voice notes, radiologic images, scanned document images, Word, Excel, and PowerPoint are improved.

Some organizations focus their IG efforts on securing confidential information by identifying PII and protected health information (PHI) and applying security software and techniques. Using **file analysis, classification, and remediation** (FACR) software finding all incidences of ePII and ePHI is easy, due to the unique characteristics of the data. Then various encryption tactics are applied.

Other healthcare organizations are focused on reducing runaway litigation discovery costs, and concentrate their efforts on e-discovery, by not only cutting ROT and organizing e-documents, which cuts costs and improves search capabilities, but also by leveraging newer technologies such as predictive coding to automate and drastically reduce document review and costs.

And yet other healthcare organizations focus on data governance as a strong component of their IG program. Improved data governance can improve data quality, data integrity, patient care, and outcomes. Data governance can also yield cost savings by data scrubbing, data cleansing, de-duplicating, and implementing master data management (MDM) to eliminate corrupted and duplicated data. In addition, new business insights can be gained on this cleaned data by using data analytics, business intelligence (BI), trend analysis, and other tools. These new insights can lead to increased revenue from upselling and cross-selling existing patients and customers, and finding new ones or creating new products or services.

The point is, there are multiple entry points for IG programs, and the focus of the effort depends on where the organization decides to invest resources. The focus of an IG program is often born out of the greatest pain points of risk and cost that boil up to the executive suite and demand attention. After their major breach, it is taken for granted that Anthem Health is now investing resources in identifying and securing ePHI and other confidential and sensitive information.

But what do all IG programs have in common as their most critical factor to succeed? What absolutely must be done before the program has a chance to succeed?

It is not running FACR software to identify PHI, duplicates, and out-of-date documents, and to begin broad classification of files, and insert basic metadata tags. No, that all sounds complicated but they are very straightforward processes. Simple software execution.

And it isn't implementing an **enterprise content management** (ECM) system or **enterprise file sync and share** (EFSS) aimed at reducing or eliminating shared drives and implementing a holistic approach to content management. That is what the software was designed to do. It manages content. Sure, many ECM efforts have failed but not because of the software itself lacked capability, but rather, poor implementation planning, training, and communications efforts have been the primary cause.

And it is not even implementing an **electronic health record** (EHR) system or other patient-centered digital technologies.

What all IG programs must do well to succeed, the *absolute most critical elements*, are firstly strong executive sponsorship. Without a long-term commitment to the IG program it will fail. But also what is often overlooked is often referred to as "soft stuff." Soft stuff includes such activities and tasks as leadership, executive communications, team selection and building, group dynamics, change management, program communications, and training. All are critical program management functions. These are the crucial elements that any IG program must include—and do well—to succeed.

Now consider the fact that IG programs must be ongoing, so it must be considered how to keep team members motivated and performing over a span of years. How will they maintain their focus for three, four, five years or more? And instill commitment to the IG program in any team replacements or additions? These are challenging tasks. They are not easy to do, which is why many IG programs will fail, leaving careers in their wake.

As a starting point, let us examine some of the considerations for determining the best executive sponsor to drive an IG program.

What is needed is to get all the varying agendas and business objectives out on the table and to assess and prioritize them according to the organization's overall business objectives. That means nominating the most senior of the potential executive sponsors to be the executive sponsor for the IG program, with a "deputy sponsor" or "supporting sponsor" as backup.

So if there is a scenario where the General Counsel, CIO, SVP of Operations, and CFO all are on board to help drive the program, perhaps the best choice is an executive who they all report up through. It could be the Administrator, or, say, the EVP of Risk Management. After all, risk is a key impact area for IG programs: Reduce the risk that PHI is breached, reduce the risk that confidential documents or IP are breached, reduce the risk that litigation costs soar out of control and threaten the brand and viability of the organization.

Key players on the IG steering committee will have differing agendas and objectives. It is essential to harmonize and prioritize the objectives of the IG program to best serve the organization.

Anticipating Conflicts in Your IG Program

By Robert F. Smallwood

There is a lot of theory in IG. The profession has been seen as "mushy" or "amorphous" but has started to firm up as case studies flow in and principles and Best Practices evolve. There have been many failures, although IG program efforts are, in fact, getting off the ground, expanding, and showing benefits in the healthcare sector.

However, few executives and managers really grasp the level of planning and effort that is required to anticipate and overcome the inherent conflicts that will arise in all IG programs.

These conflicts are inevitable due to the cross-functional nature that is essential for IG program efforts. Think about it: usually the typical hierarchical organization is structured by business functions and those at the top of the ladder in C-level positions can set objectives and drive results through their direct reports. These executives are tough people who fought their way up the ladder.

However, IG programs require that these steely C-level executives from key functional areas (including legal, IT privacy, security, risk management, and him, and perhaps more depending on the organization) work together and collaborate.

Stop and think about that for a minute.

Consider the politics and competition that is a part of every organization. The CIO and CFO and General Counsel and others at that level are all competing to get that next promotion to executive VP, COO, or even CEO.

Competition at that level is fierce. IG can be a full contact sport!

So here we have the rub, the crux of the matter, the reason why many IG programs lose steam and fail.

They are sabotaged for political purposes, often slowly and covertly, by those not leading the effort, or those who have the least to gain by its success. Since there are so many moving parts to an IG program, simple dragging of feet or missing a few meetings can start to kill the effort.

Smart and successful IG practitioners will be aware of the inherent conflicts in political agendas, business objectives, and careers, and build in conflict resolution and change management tactics to their IG program strategies.

Information Governance and Brand Management: A Critical Link

By Robert F. Smallwood

Brand management is a critical impact area of IG programs. Protecting the value of an organization's brand is of paramount importance to stockholders and stakeholders. Most healthcare organizations in the U.S. are for-profit so their brand and image matters.

During the Chipotle Mexican Grill food poisoning outbreaks of late 2015, the stock dropped over 40% in just three months. That's around $5 billion in value. That is real money. $5 billion that vanished due to the reputational damage wrought on the Chipotle brand. Damage that was caused by poor recordkeeping and a lack of good information for management to analyze: essentially a failure of IG. And the stock price never completely recovered.

So executives and marketing departments also have a stake in IG, particularly in large public companies.

Information Governance by Design: "Baking" IG into Everyday Processes

By Robert F. Smallwood

The goal of IG programs is to continuously strive to change the organizational culture and underlying business processes so that IG considerations including information security, privacy, legality, records and health information management (HIM), e-discovery readiness, and information quality are an everyday, routine part of managing information.

Leading IG practitioners call this process of infusing IG into business processes the "routinizing" of IG. Once these IG considerations become a routine part of operations—"baked in" to them, you might say—the organization will have achieved, in a sense, *IG by Design* XE "Information Governance:IG by Design" .

IG by Design means that critical privacy and security considerations and requirements become a part of everyday, routine business processes, as do regulatory and legal considerations, information quality assurance, HIM requirements, and IT efficiency considerations, all focused on maximizing information value while minimizing information risks and costs. This redesign requires deep knowledge of the organization's IG goals and strategies, and business process analysis (BPA) to redesign and streamline processes while baking in IG considerations. Then IG-enabling information technologies should be evaluated and deployed when justified and in alignment with IT strategy and business objectives. These technologies will help to monitor and enforce IG policies.

The result of IG by Design is reduced risks: lessened information risk, privacy risk, legal risk, and compliance risks while improving information value, which leads to greater profitability and viability for the business.

But it takes vision and leadership to pull off. Most organizations are far away from the IG by Design ideal. For those just starting down the path, it is best to form business objectives, recruit an executive sponsor, and draft an IG steering committee. Then draw up the overall program and select target areas where some early wins can show real results.

If large regulatory fines have been levied due to a HIPAA audit, then business processes must be re-evaluated and more employee training should be done with the business objective of reducing and eventually eliminating these fines. This process must start from the beginning with a thorough yet expedient inventorying of information assets, and, better yet, creating an Information Asset Register (IAR) to track and monitor information assets.

IG by Design as a term may be a little misleading since it implies that once the design is set, the organization has "achieved" IG. However, IG is an ongoing, "evergreen" program that evolves and expands and pushes to continuously improve.

Striving for IG by Design should be a paramount goal of any IG program. From there, with leadership, training, communications, reinforcement, solid metrics, and a prudent audit process, adjustments and improvements can continue to be made.

Veteran Advice on Getting Your IG Program Launched

By Richard P. Kessler

When first developing an IG program, corporate executives should be wary to keep its initial scope narrow, carefully select the right people as its initial contributors, and create a framework that supports growth and future success.

Early "wins" are key to an IG program's long-term survival. The first IG project must be selected with care so it can be accomplished relatively quickly while also delivering demonstrable value. For example, a proposed project that requires new technology to be rapidly developed, evaluated, approved, and implemented to realize a time-sensitive, significant, revenue-generating opportunity can provide an excellent opportunity to demonstrate the value of the IG approach. In such cases, IG can be used to facilitate a coordinated, collaborative, and parallel review by SMEs within legal, litigation, compliance, operational risk, IT, HR, regulatory, and information security, and other functions that may normally work serially, separately, or worse, *at cross-purposes.* An IG program can be used to create a governance structure that coordinates these different roles. This can be a great place to start if you do not have a specific, significant, and recent incident to leverage.

If you have recently had an event that challenged your organization and perhaps resulted in damaging press or a significant drop in stock price, it often can be leveraged to start an IG program. A data security breach, regulatory fine, lawsuit, or other significant loss can jumpstart an IG program. It will bring together an initial set of SMEs, and serve as an opportunity for the right leader to step in and coordinate and address the incident or resulting challenge.

An experienced executive will already know how vital a dedicated, empowered, and funded senior executive sponsor is to any program. However, a fledgling program—especially an IG program—*also requires a strong, intelligent, patient, and well-spoken leader.* This person should be a subject matter expert in several IG disciplines, such as records management, eDiscovery, security, and IT, and have a working knowledge of related subject areas to enable issue spotting as challenges arise. They will need to rapidly understand and resolve conflicts and differences of opinion among both contributors and governance-body members alike.

The leader must also create an environment of mutual respect, understanding, collaboration, and open communication, so that minority and dissenting opinions are welcomed and no one is afraid to speak when they see an issue for their particular discipline. Foster an environment of discussion and "give and take," even if it means getting a bit off track from a meeting's purpose—this will facilitate a sense of contribution and ownership that will increase the group's effectiveness better than a rigid adherence to pre-set agendas. This same individual will then need to lead the group to a defensible and actionable decision, and create consensus for the best possible way forward. This is not easy to do, and early experiences with smaller groups will be vital so that the leader can learn from their mistakes. The process to figure out, actually "feel" out, how to manage the governance structure appropriately is an iterative one and will require patience and a willingness to adjust your approach as you go. For example, getting to a "perfect" way forward often will not be possible. A good leader will help the IG team understand that the perfect can be the enemy of the good, and that a risk-value-cost balance will often be the best achievable result.

Even with a strong leader, it is critical that the IG steering committee be comprised of strong SMEs that also have the right level of authority and responsibility within the firm. In IG, it is often all about the details, and the members of the team must understand the nuances of their field. Thus, early iterations of an IG program should include a relatively small group of stakeholders that are patient with each other, have some knowledge outside their own discipline, and can communicate well. Ideally, these people should include challengers and contributors. Diversity of opinion and perspective and the resulting challenges will help the team identify the best way forward, and contributors will help map out the path to get there.

As the scope of the IG program expands and the repeatable success becomes a reality, principles and strategic objectives of the program should be developed to serve as the constraints and guideposts for the IG team. *Creation of IG guidelines, standards, and exception procedures are vital to resolve conflicts, which will inevitably arise.* There will be times when not everyone will agree and consensus will seem unattainable; having standards and principles in place will help get and keep everyone on track.

In summary, by leveraging the right initial project or program, carefully selecting leaders and SMEs with the right mix of attributes, strong executive sponsorship, and a principled framework supporting further growth and expansion, your nascent IG program will not only get off the ground but will be poised for success and integration into every facet of your organization's change efforts.

Notes

1. GDPR Article 37(1)(a–c).
2. GDPR Article 37(3).
3. GDPR Article 38(1–3).
4. GDPR Article 38(4–6).
5. Article 29 Working Group (2016), *Guidelines on Data Protection Officer*, fn. 34, pp. 15–16.
6. Article 29 Working Group (2016), p. 15.
7. GDPR Article 37(5).
8. GDPR Recital 97.
9. Article 29 Working Group (2016), p. 11.
10. Article 29 Working Group (2016), pp. 13–14.
11. For illustrative purposes, at time of writing, an NHS Band 8a member of staff earned between £40,428 and £48,514. This figure is based on a candid belief of the salary the role is realistically likely to attract, rather than what it is truly worth.

Glossary

Archive: Storing information and records for long-term or permanent preservation. With respect to e-mail, in a compressed and indexed format to reduce storage requirements and allow for rapid, complex searches (this can also be done for blogs, social media, or other applications). Archiving of real-time applications like e-mail can only be deemed reliable with record integrity if it is performed immediately, in real time.

AHIMA: American Health Information Management Association, the U.S.-based nonprofit organization for health information managers which has been prominent in the development and promotion of IG in the U.S.

ARMA: Association for Records Managers and Administrators, the U.S.-based nonprofit organization for records managers with a network of international chapters.

Auto-classification: Setting pre-defined indices to classify documents and records and have the process performed automatically by using software, rather than human intervention. A strong trend toward auto-classification is emerging due to the impact of "Big Data" and rapidly increasing volumes of documents and records.

Backup: A complete spare copy of data for purposes of disaster recovery. Backups are non-indexed mass storage and cannot substitute for indexed, archived information that can be quickly searched and retrieved (as in archiving).

Case records: Case records are characterized as having a beginning and an end, but are added to over time. Case records generally have titles that include names, dates, numbers, or places.

Classification: Systematic identification and arrangement of business activities and/or records into categories according to logically structured conventions, methods, and procedural rules represented in a classification system. A coding of content items as members of a group for the purposes of cataloging them or associating them with a taxonomy.

Cloud computing: Cloud computing refers to the provision of computational resources on demand via a network. Cloud computing can be compared to the supply of a utility like electricity, water, or gas, or the provision of telephone or television services. All of these services are presented to the users in a simple way that is easy to understand without the users' needing to know how the services are provided. This simplified view is called an abstraction. Similarly, cloud computing offers computer application developers and users an abstract view of services, which simplifies and ignores many of the details and inner workings. A provider's offering of abstracted Internet services is often called The Cloud.

Code of Federal Regulations: "The Code of Federal Regulations (CFR)" annual edition is the codification of the general and permanent rules published in the Federal Register by the departments and agencies of the federal government. It is divided into 50 titles that represent broad areas subject to federal regulation. The 50 subject matter titles contain one or more individual volumes, which are updated once each calendar year, on a staggered basis."[1]

Cold site:　A cold site is simply an empty computer facility or data center that is ready with air conditioning, raised floors, telecommunication lines, and electric power. Backup hardware and software will have to be purchased and shipped in quickly to resume operations. Arrangements can be made with suppliers for rapid delivery in the event of a disaster.

Dark data:　Data that is unknown in nature, or difficult to identify due to a lack of metadata.

Data loss prevention (DLP):　Data loss prevention (DLP; also known as data *leak* prevention) is a computer security term referring to systems that identify, monitor, and protect data in use (e.g. endpoint actions), data in motion (e.g. network actions), and data at rest (e.g. data storage) through deep content inspection, contextual security analysis of transaction (attributes of originator, data object, medium, timing, recipient/destination, and so on) and with a centralized management framework. Systems are designed to detect and prevent unauthorized use and transmission of confidential information.

Destruction certificate:　Issued once the destruction of a record is complete, which verifies it has taken place, who authorized the destruction, and who carried it out. May include some metadata about the record.

Destructive retention policy:　Permanently destroying documents or e-documents (such as e-mail) after retaining them for a specified period of time.

Disaster recovery (DR)/business continuity (BC):　The planning, preparation, and testing set of activities used to help a business plan for and recover from any major business interruption and to resume normal business operations.

Discovery:　May refer to the process of gathering and exchanging evidence in civil trials; or, to discovering information flows inside an organization using data loss prevention (DLP) tools.

Disposition:　The range of processes associated with implementing records retention, destruction, or transfer decisions, which are documented in disposition authorities or other instruments.

Document analytics:　Detailed usage statistics on e-documents, such as time spent viewing, which pages were viewed and for how long, number of documents printed, where printed, number of copies printed, and other granular information about how and where a document is accessed, viewed, edited, or printed.

Document lifecycle:　The span of a document's use, from creation, through active use, storage, and final disposition, which may be destruction or preservation.

Document lifecycle security (DLS):　Providing a secure and controlled environment for e-documents. This can be accomplished by properly implementing technologies including information rights management (IRM) and data loss prevention (DLP), along with complementary technologies like digital signatures.

Document management:　Managing documents throughout their lifecycle from creation to final disposition, including managing revisions. Also called document lifecycle management.

Electronic document and records management system (EDRMS):　Software that has the ability to manage documents and records electronically, including physical records.

Electronically stored information (ESI):　A term coined by the legal community to connote any information at all that is stored by electronic means; this can include not just e-mail and e-documents but also audio and video recordings, and any other type of information stored on electronic media. ESI is a term that was created in 2006 when the U.S. Federal Rules of Civil Procedure (FRCP) were revised to include the governance of ESI in litigation.

E-mail and e-document encryption: E-mail and e-document encryption refers to encryption or scrambling (and often authentication) of e-mail messages, which can be done in order to protect the content from being read by unintended recipients.

Enterprise content management (ECM): Software that manages unstructured information such as e-documents, document images, e-mail, word processing documents, spreadsheets, Web content, and other documents; most systems also include some records management capability.

Enterprise process analytics: Detailed statistics and analysis of business process cycle times and other data occurring throughout an enterprise. This business intelligence can help spot bottlenecks, optimize workflow, and improve worker productivity while improving input for decision-making.

Event-based disposition: A disposition instruction in which a record is eligible for the specified disposition (transfer or destroy) when or immediately after the specified event occurs. No retention period is applied and there is no fixed waiting period as with timed or combination timed-event dispositions. Example: *Destroy when no longer needed for current operations.*

Federal Rules of Civil Procedure (FRCP)—Amended 2006: In U.S. civil litigation, the FRCP governs the discovery and exchange of electronically stored information (ESI), which includes not only e-mail but all forms of information that can be stored electronically.

File plan: A file plan is a graphic representation of the business classification scheme (BCS), usually a "hierarchical structure consisting of headings and folders to indicate where and when records should be created during the conducting of the business of an office. In other words the file plan links the records to their business context."

Generally Accepted Recordkeeping Principles®: A set of eight Generally Accepted Recordkeeping Principles®, also known as "The Principles" within the records management community,[2] published in 2009 by U.S.-based ARMA International to foster awareness of good recordkeeping practices and to provide guidance for records management maturity in organizations. These principles and associated metrics provide an **information governance** (IG) framework that can support continuous improvement.

HIPAA: The Healthcare Insurance Portability and Accountability Act (HIPAA) was enacted by the U.S. Congress in 1996. According to the Centers for Medicare and Medicaid Services (CMS) website, Title II of HIPAA, known as the administrative simplification (AS) provision, requires the establishment of national standards for electronic healthcare transactions and national identifiers for providers, health insurance plans, and employers.

Hot site: A hot site is one that has identical or nearly identical hardware and operating system configurations and copies of application software, and receives live, real-time backup data from business operations. In the event of a business interruption, the operations can be switched over automatically, providing uninterrupted service.

Information governance (IG): IG is "security, control, and optimization" of information. IG is an ongoing program that helps organizations meet external compliance and legal demands and internal governance rules. IG minimizes information risks and costs while maximizing its value.

Information lifecycle: The span of the use of information, from creation, through active use, storage, and final disposition, which may be destruction or preservation.

Information rights management (IRM): Information rights management (IRM) applies to a technology set that protects sensitive information, usually documents or e-mail messages, from unauthorized access. IRM is technology that allows for information (mostly in the form of documents) to be encrypted and remotely controlled. This means that information and its control can be separately created, viewed, edited, and distributed.

Limitation period: The length of time after which a legal action cannot be brought before the courts. Limitation periods are important because they determine the length of time records must be kept to support court action (including subsequent appeal periods). It is important to be familiar with the purpose, principles, and special circumstances that affect limitation periods and therefore records retention."[3]

Long-term digital preservation: The managed activities, methods, standards, and technologies used to provide long-term, error-free storage of digital information, with means for retrieval and interpretation, for the entire time span the information is required to be retained.

Phishing: Phishing is a way of attempting to acquire sensitive information such as user names, passwords, and credit card details by masquerading as a trustworthy entity in an electronic communication. Communications purporting to be from popular social websites, auction sites, online payment processors, or IT administrators are commonly used to lure the unsuspecting public. Phishing is typically carried out by e-mail or instant messaging, and it often directs users to enter details at a fake website that looks and feels almost identical to the legitimate one. Phishing is an example of social engineering techniques used to fool users, and it exploits the poor usability of current web security technologies.

Policy: A high-level overall plan, containing a set of principles that embrace the general goals of the organization and are used as a basis for decisions. Can include some specifics of processes allowed and not allowed.

Preservation: The processes and operations involved in ensuring the technical and intellectual survival of authentic records through time.

Records appraisal: The process of assessing the value and risk of records to determine their retention and disposition requirements. Legal research is outlined in appraisal reports. This may be accomplished as a part of the process of developing the records retention schedules, as well as conducting a regular review to ensure that citations and requirements are current.

Records integrity: Refers to the accuracy and consistency of records, and the assurance that they are genuine and unaltered.

Records retention schedule: A records retention schedule spells out how long different types of records are to be held, and how they will be archived or disposed of at the end of their lifecycle. It contains regulatory citations and considers legal, regulatory, operational, and historical requirements.

ROT: Redundant, outdated, or trivial information that should be identified and deleted to improve operational efficiencies.

Spoliation: The loss of proven authenticity of a record. Can occur in the case of e-mail records if they are not captured in real time, or they have been edited in any way.

Structured information: Information in databases; organized data.

Taxonomy: A hierarchical structure of information components, for example, a subject, business unit, or functional taxonomy, any part of which can be used to classify a content item in relation to other items in the structure.

Text mining: Performing detailed full-text searches on the content of document.

Thesaurus: In taxonomies, a thesaurus contains all synonyms and definitions and is used to enforce naming conventions in a controlled vocabulary; for example, *invoice* and *bill* could be terms that are used interchangeably.

Total cost of ownership (TCO): All costs associated with owning a hardware and software system over the life of the implementation—usually considered over a range of three to five years. TCO includes implementation price and change orders (and the change order approval process), which occur when changes to the project are made outside of the original proposal. Timing and pricing of the software support fees are also critical TCO components, and may include warranty periods, annual fees, planned and maximum increases, trade-in and upgrade costs, hardware maintenance costs, and other charges.

Unstructured information: Information that lacks metadata, or has little metadata, such as e-mail, Word documents, PowerPoint slides, scanned images, PDFs, and the like. Information not expressed in numerical rows and columns but, rather, as objects. Structured records are maintained in databases.

Vital records: Vital records are mission-critical records that are necessary for an organization to continue to operate in the event of disruption or disaster and cannot be recreated from any other source. Sometimes referred to as critical information assets. Typically, they make up about 3%–5% of an organization's total records. They are the most important records to be protected, and a plan for disaster recovery (DR)/business continuity (BC) must be in place to safeguard these records.

Warm site: A warm site may have all (or mostly all) identical hardware and operating systems, such as a hot site does, and software licenses for the same applications, and needs only to have data loaded to resume normal operations. Internal IT staff may have to retrieve magnetic tapes, optical disks, or other storage media containing the most recent backup data, and some data may be lost if the backup is not real time and continuous.

Notes

1. "Code of Federal Regulations," U.S. Government Publishing Office (GPO), https://www.gpo.gov/fdsys/browse/collectionCfr.action?collectionCode=CFR.
2. "Generally Accepted Recordkeeping Principles®," ARMA International, http://www.arma.org/docs/sharepoint-roadshow/the-principles_executive-summaries_final.doc.
3. "Developing Retention and Disposition Schedules," Government of Alberta, p. 122.

Index

Printed in the United States
by Baker & Taylor Publisher Services